**LILLIAN TOO &
JENNIFER TOO**

2011

fortune & feng shui

Snake

Congratulations!

I want to thank and congratulate you for investing in yourself...and in the latest edition of Fortune and Feng Shui...your personalized horoscope book for 2011!

What will you be earning one year from today? How will you look and feel one year from today...and will you be happier?

In this little book Jennifer and I reveal many insights pertaining to your particular animal sign...what you can expect and how to protect and enhance all areas of your life for success in 2011.

And why stop here?

I'd like to also extend a personal invitation to you to join my Mandala...and receive my FREE online weekly newsletter...Lillian Too's Mandala Ezine.

You'll discover other powerful feng shui secrets from me that go hand-in-hand with the valuable information in this book. And it's absolutely FREE... delivered to your inbox weekly!

Fortune & Feng Shui 2011 SNAKE
by Lillian Too and Jennifer Too
© 2011 Konsep Lagenda Sdn Bhd

Text © 2011 Lillian Too and Jennifer Too
Photographs and illustrations © WOFS.com Sdn Bhd

The moral right of the authors to be identified as authors of this book
has been asserted.

Published by KONSEP LAGENDA SDN BHD (223 855)
Kuala Lumpur 59100 Malaysia

For more Konsep books, go to www.lillian-too.com or www.wofs.com
To report errors, please send a note to errors@konsepbooks.com
For general feedback, email feedback@konsepbooks.com

ISBN 978-967-329-044-4
Published in Malaysia, August 2010

SNAKE BORN CHART

BIRTH YEAR	WESTERN CALENDAR DATES	AGE	KUA NUMBER MALES	KUA NUMBER FEMALES
Earth Snake	10 Feb 1929 to 29 Jan 1930	82	8 West Group	7 West Group
Metal Snake	27 Jan 1941 to 14 Feb 1942	70	5 West Group	1 East Group
Water Snake	14 Feb 1953 to 2 Feb 1954	58	2 West Group	4 East Group
Wood Snake	2 Feb 1965 to 20 Jan 1966	46	8 West Group	7 West Group
Fire Snake	18 Feb 1977 to 6 Feb 1978	34	5 West Group	1 East Group
Earth Snake	6 Feb 1989 to 26 Jan 1990	22	2 West Group	4 East Group
Metal Snake	24 Jan 2001 to 11 Feb 2002	10	8 West Group	7 West Group

CONTENTS

4. INTERACTING WITH OTHERS IN 2010
Up Close, Snake's Bright Charisma
Seems Irresistible

5. MONTHLY ANALYSES OF YOUR LUCK
Snake Goes Through
A Magical High Energy Year

6. IMPORTANT FENG SHUI UPDATES FOR 2011

7. POWERFUL TALISMANS & AMULETS FOR 2011

RABBIT YEAR 2011
Clashing Elements
But Economically Better

The year of the Golden Rabbit 2011 will be a noisy year filled with the sounds of clashing elements. Global energy continues to be discordant. But it is a year when most of the animal signs enjoy the potential to make genuinely good advances economically. There is money to be made.

In fact, for those who are able to tap into their veins of good fortune, 2011 can turn out to be a bonanza year. It is a year that favors animal signs located in the secondary compass directions and is less favorable to those occupying cardinal directions. So two thirds of the animal signs can look forward to improving their financial situation.

We examine three important indicators to determine the year's outlook when the diplomatic, soft-hearted Rabbit rules, taking center stage and bringing a new set of energies to the fortunes of the world. After the dramatic earthquakes, landslides & volcanic eruptions of the Tiger Year, can we welcome in a quieter, safer and more stable year? Alas, if the charts are any indication, it seems not; there are deep rumblings under the earth; natural disasters and discordant chi continues to pose a threat to our safety; these calamities threaten different parts of the world. Earth's environment needs time to settle but for most individuals, happily the outlook does not look that dire. There is more good luck than bad for most of the animal signs.

Outlook for the 12 Animals

In 2011, the **Snake** enters a year when a series of small successes can be effectively be transformed into big ones. There are excellent feng shui winds which bring continuous good fortune. Heaven chi awakens new horizons for you, so it should not be difficult to use special rituals and talismans to transform small into big. Good fortune comes from the 24 mountain stars as Snake sits on a *Small Auspicious* star and is flanked by one Big and one Small Auspicious star. This combines with the number 6 star in your chart and your strong inner chi essence to bring you a magnificent year.

The **Ox**, the Snake's ally also enjoys a wonderful year as it benefits from the double *Big Auspicious* stars that flank its astrological location. This together with its number 1 star ensures that good fortune manifests strongly. Meanwhile, inviting a deity figure into the home brings good luck as the Ox has the *Golden Deity Star* in its chart this year.

The **Rat** and the **Horse** also enjoy the promise of good fortune, but whether or not they can actually cause this good luck potential to materialize will depend on their own inventiveness. But doing well in 2011 does not come without a share of the year's discordance. The Horse has a tendency to get sick, while the Rat's normally calm demeanor is put out of sorts by quarrelsome impulses brought by the hostility star.

Two other animal signs enjoying excellent potential are the **Dog** and the **Boar**, although for them, success luck can diminish if they are affected by discordant forces in their personal charts or simply have outdated feng shui in the home. The Boar especially must stay updated and be careful not to get blocked by the year's afflictive energies. They should check to make sure neither their main door nor bedrooms are afflicted this year.

In 2011, both the East and West animal rulers, the **Rabbit** itself and the **Rooster** (Dragon's secret friend) must stay watchful. These two need to be mindful of their backs, as both are potentially affected by the *Disaster Energy Star* and other feng shui afflictions. The Rabbit is hit by the nasty *wu wang* or five yellow, while the Rooster sits on the *Natural Disaster Star* and must contend with the *Three Killings* affliction. So a challenging time is in store for these two signs.

The **Dragon** has a rather uneventful year. The Dragon can sail through 2011 with luck being small and success being limited, but there is little to cause them grieve. Indeed, for the Dragon, heaven luck shines bright, so there could well be unexpected windfalls. It is a good idea to enhance for special luck to manifest. For them, wearing and displaying good luck charms will help them.

The **Sheep** benefits from the year but only when there is an adequate supply of Earth element energy, so this sign needs strengthening with the **Earth Seal**. It also benefits to display and wear raw crystal and natural quartz crystal. Large reconstituted crystal globes are of benefit.

The **Monkey** (the Snake's secret friend) meanwhile has a harder time staying ahead of the competition, especially those working in a professional career. Those doing business need to watch they do not get cheated or conned. This sign must be careful not to fall victim to external politicking. The Monkey must be wary and alert to false friends and ambitious colleagues. It is beneficial to carry amulets that fight against the evil eye!

Finally, the **Tiger** must work at generating heaven luck energy by wearing the **Heaven Seal**. Doing so brings good fortune. This is a year when depending on your own instincts benefit you more than listening to others.

**Carry the Heaven Seal
Amulet** to enhance Snake's
No.6 heaven luck.

The Year's Four Pillars

The first indicator we look at to get an overall feel for the destiny outlook for the year is the year's Four Pillars chart. This offers a snapshot of the year and reveals the hidden forces that affect the fortunes of the year. To know what's in store, we analyze the eight elements that dominate the four pillars i.e. the heavenly stems and earthly branches that rule the chi energies of the year.

The preceding Tiger Year was a year of unstable earth disasters characterized by rogue waves in the seas and big earthquakes that began at the start of the year and continued unabated through the year... from Chile to Japan to Turkey to Indonesia to China and Taiwan. Last year, hidden Earth energies rumbled and brought tragedy to many parts of the globe.

In this coming year 2011 of the Golden Metallic Rabbit, its Four Pillars Chart looks rather foreboding. In fact, the chart is indicating not one pillar of directly clashing elements, but FOUR!

Yes, all four of the pillars have discordant crushing energies, with three pillars indicating Metal crushing Wood, instantly telling us that the Rabbit of 2011

PAHT CHEE CHART 2011 - GOLDEN RABBIT

HOUR	DAY	MONTH	YEAR
HEAVENLY STEM	HEAVENLY STEM	HEAVENLY STEM	HEAVENLY STEM
壬	庚	庚	辛
YANG WATER	YANG METAL	YANG METAL	YIN METAL
EARTHLY BRANCH	EARTHLY BRANCH	EARTHLY BRANCH	EARTHLY BRANCH
丙午	甲寅	甲寅	乙卯
FIRE HORSE	WOOD TIGER	WOOD TIGER	WOOD RABBIT

HIDDEN HEAVENLY STEMS OF THE YEAR

YANG FIRE YANG EARTH	YANG FIRE YANG EARTH YANG WOOD	YANG FIRE YANG EARTH YANG WOOD	YIN WOOD

The year is desperately short of EARTH ie Resource

is not going to be a docile one. The remaining pillar has **Water destroying Fire**. So in 2011, all four pillars that make up the Eight Characters chart of the year are showing direct clashes. This is a nasty indication and it is a clear warning for everyone to be careful and circumspect.

Travel and risk-taking are best kept to a minimum, and it is a good idea to be prepared at all times. It is not a year to tempt fate. This is a general but potent piece of advice for the year. Better to stay home than to travel. Better to stay safe than to take risks. Just glance quickly at the chart and instantly you will see that in the DAY, MONTH and YEAR pillars, Metal is destroying Wood! These are direct clashes and here we see both yin and yang pillars having the same clashing characteristics.

And then in the HOUR pillar, Water is destroying Fire! Each one of the four pillars indicates extremely negative outlooks for the year; so from year start to year end, and affecting all age groups, hostile energies dominate. This has to be a record of some kind; to have all four pillars showing a clash of elements with the heavenly stem elements destroying the earthly branches in every single pillar of the chart.

Disharmony is thus the prominent force of the coming year and despite the Rabbit, usually an icon of diplomacy, it appears that feng shui cosmic forces this year bring plenty of high octane anger and intolerance. In addition, the chart also show the presence of two Tigers, which suggests that the Tiger energies of 2010 have not entirely abated. We face a scenario not unlike that of the previous year, but maybe worse; clashing elements are always indicators of hard times, so the energy of the year looks discordant.

The chart shows Metal and Wood dominating, with Metal energy having the upper hand. The essence of the year is Metal, but it is neither weak nor strong Metal. Although we see three Metal, the Water and Fire of the HOUR pillar destroys and weakens the Metal. And because there is no Earth element present in the chart, Metal lacks the resources to stay strong.

There appears then to be a lack of resources during the year, and this of course is another bad sign. The absence of Earth also suggests an unbalanced chart, which is also an indication of turmoil.

With this obvious imbalance, the prevailing attitude during the year is one of unrelenting intolerance. There are three Metals indicating the presence of competitive pressures, but the strength of the Metals cannot be sustained because of the lack of Earth. This indicates that competitive pressures cannot be sustained and it is best to not be pushed into a corner by competitors. Try thinking outside the box instead of combating the competition!

The Good News

However, when we look at the hidden elements of the chart, the news for 2011 is not all bad. Underlying all the competing energy lies the potential for the creation of much new wealth. There is hidden Earth bringing unexpected resources to fuel growth for the year, and there is also hidden Wood, indicating unexpected wealth.

Likewise, there is also hidden Fire, so the year does not lack for managerial capability. The exercise of authority and leadership plays a big role in transforming the cosmic forces in 2011. Results may not be evident in the year itself, but there is no denying the positive benefits of good leadership. As the NW patriarchal sector this year has the 8, the cosmic forces are aligned to help the patriarchs i.e. the leaders of the planet. So in the trinity of heaven, earth and man, *tien ti ren*, it will be Mankind energy that prevails and delivers success and results.

> Herein lies the good news for those who are commercially minded and business motivated. 2011 is a year when plenty of prosperity-making opportunities are present. There are many direct as well as indirect wealth-making opportunities emerging.

Although what is apparently missing are direct resources as indicated by the element Earth, which is missing from the main chart, there are thankfully three hidden Earth element. This more than makes up for their absence in the main chart. In effect, the chart can now be said to be balanced with the presence of all five elements when the hidden elements are taken into account.

> What is in very small supply however is the element of **Water**, which was completely missing last year.

In 2011, Water represents creativity, intelligence and common sense. Because it is in such short supply, everyone once again continues to benefit from the **Water** element. This is what will create Wood which stands for wealth this year. Water also exhausts Metal which is destroying the Wood element.

Thus the source of wealth creation in 2011 is Water; i.e. creativity - original and strategic thinking which will open the way to mining the year's prosperity. Much of this creativity will come from the younger generation.

This will be a year when those who have just joined the workforce, and those who have recently graduated out of school and college will be the source of new ideas. And because it is the year of the Rabbit, when the East sector comes into prominence, it is likely that those born as the eldest sons of their families will be the ones whose stars will shine brightly. This year benefits the eldest sons of families.

Rabbit Years have always been years of appeasement, when conflicts arising in preceding Tiger Years get resolved. Unfortunately, 2011 continues to be a year of global political upheavals.

For the Snake-born however, there are no direct or personal conflicts to contend with. You will have a really good year as there are plenty of good feng shui winds helping you.

The Golden Rabbit Year is challenging and full of intrigues. Unlike the direct confrontations of the previous year, this is a year when unexpected betrayals and underhand tactics will be prevalent.

For the Snake sign, you should just ignore all the power plays and political intrigues going on under your nose; they cannot hurt you as your chi is very strong. Those feeling this darker side of the year's energy need to have a positive and non-defeatist attitude; only then can the coming twelve months from February 4th 2011 to February 4th 2012 benefit you. Then in spite of discordant element indications, you can create and accumulate new assets.

There is wealth luck in 2011. The Snake is definately able to harness wealth luck as you are surrounded by excellent 24 mountain influences. What is needed is a keen eye for opportunities. Think outside the box to create new markets for your service and your products. The global business scenario is changing fast. New technology and applications of this fast-developing new technology is racing ahead at breakneck speed.

Globally, there is more than one prominent player in the technology game. Increasingly, the world is feeling the presence of China. Note that Period 7 benefitted the West, but it is the Northeast that is ruling the energies of the current Period 8. This Period favors China.

Both the year 2011 and the Period itself favors those who move fast and who have prepared themselves to penetrate uncharted territory, just like water. We borrow the term blue oceans to suggest the clever opening up of new areas for creating wealth. And it does not matter whether you live in the West or in the Northeast, if you can work with the cosmic forces of the year and the period, you are sure to benefit.

Water is Vital

This is once again a year when the element of Water will lead to prosperity, although not in the same way it did in the previous year. But those of you who installed water features last year and benefited from them will again harness good luck from the water. Note that in 2011, we are seeing three Metal destroying three Wood - i.e. clashing directly. The **Metal** of the year's heavenly stems continuing to destroy the Tiger's intrinsic **Wood**. On the surface this is not a good sign.

But Metal, when used with skill and under special circumstances, can transform Wood into something of greater value. So even as Metal destroys Wood, it can transform Wood into an object of value. What is great this year is that there is more than enough Wood to make up for whatever gets destroyed. Note from the Pillars chart there are 3 hidden Wood, so there is definitely wealth to be created and accumulated.

But clashing elements always suggest hostilities, so the wars of the world will not see any easing or closure.
In 2011, fighting continues with little hope for reconciliation; competition in the commercial environment and between companies and countries get worse.

Mankind energy can be harnessed very effectively to overcome the discordant energies of heaven and earth this year. All the resources required are available, the only snag being they are hidden and so, not immediately obvious. But they are there!

So here we can use the third dimension of feng shui - the powerful inner chi dimension - to transform and enhance the space and time chi of 2011 at individual personalized levels. Irrespective of the discordance of Heaven and Earth, those of us who know how can still arrange our lives to benefit from the hidden forces of the year. We can focus on the mankind chi within all of us - focus on strengthening it - and in so doing, more effectively harness the spiritual energy of the empowered self to overcome obstacles and emerge triumphant.

There are methods and rituals we can use to subdue negative energies caused by the four sets of clashing elements. We can also apply element therapy to bring about a much improved balance in the elements in our immediate environments; and there are symbolic cures, many made into amulets, that can subdue negative "*stars*".

The Commanding Star

A very positive aspect of the year 2011 is the appearance of the *Commanding Star,* an outstandingly auspicious star. Its appearance in the 2011 chart is brought about by the presence of the Earthly Branch of Horse in the Hour pillar and the Earthly branch of Tiger in the Day pillar. This excellent indication arises out of the ally relationship that exists between Horse and Tiger. Here, the Commanding Star suggests traits brought by these two fearless animal signs to the year. It brings good vibrations benefiting those who show courage and fortitude.

The Commanding Star suggests the presence of authority, power and influence luck for the year, benefiting those who find themselves in a leadership situation or those holding a position of authority.

Indeed, the year will benefit those who know how to use their positions of influence and power; so managers and leaders who have a clear idea what their strategy or focus are will benefit from this star, despite the clashing elements of the year. Leaders will find the energy of the year increases their charisma and their effectiveness. The exercise of authority will come easily, and for those who also enjoy auspicious stars such as those of you of the Snake sign. You can rejoice because you have three stars of the 24 mountains bringing you lots of very auspicious luck, big as well as small; so for you the year looks very promising.

As such you, the Snake person can consider developing new markets, or trying out a different strategy or even investing in a new venture. You also enjoy the feng shui star of 6, so the year brings exciting opportunities. What is needed for you to take advantage of 2011 energy is your own confidence, which thankfully you have in spades this year.

What can however be worrying about the Commanding Star is that both the elements of the Hour pillar - Water and Fire - are not good for the intrinsic element of the year. Here we see Fire destroying Metal, and Water exhausting Metal. Superficially then, it appears that the Commanding Star can turn ugly, bringing obstacles instead of opportunities.

Flying Stars of 2011

The feng shui chart of the year, which lays out the location of the year's flying stars in 2011 is dominated by the energy of 7, a weak star; but being the reigning number, its effect cannot be overlooked. The number 7 is a Metal number that represents the negative side of relationships, symbolizing duplicity and treachery. The number adds fuel to the discordant vibes of the clashing elements of the Four Pillars. So while the Rabbit Year is usually a more subdued year, 2011 will see a tendency to confrontation, and violence is likely to continue. This is a year when intrigue and situational upheavals occur more frequently than usual; these are brought about by a higher occurrence of betrayals and unbridled ambitions. It is a year when the center of buildings, houses and offices benefit from the presence of Water energy to subdue the strength of the 7.

Luckily, the number 7 is a weak star in the current Period of 8, so it is not difficult to subdue it. Anything of a dark blue color would be sufficient for keeping it under control. It is advisable to make the effort to suppress the number 7 in homes and offices. This will ensure protection for residents against falling victim to external politicking and trouble-making people.

In 2011 it is beneficial to activate the power of Water in the home. Invest in a small water feature to create a small presence of moving water in the center grid of the home. Or you can place a **Rhino** or **Elephant** there. Together, these three remedies are excellent for suppressing the negative influence of 7.

The luck of the different sectors of any structure is influenced by the new energy brought by the year's feng shui chart, as this reveals the year's lucky and unlucky sectors for buildings, houses and apartments.

FLYING STAR CHART 2011 - GOLDEN RABBIT

SE	SOUTH	SW
SMALL AUSPICIOUS **6** SMALL AUSPICIOUS	BIG AUSPICIOUS **2** BIG AUSPICIOUS	EARTH SEAL **4** ROBBERY STAR
TAI SUI **5** 5 YELLOW	**7**	**9** 3 KILLINGS
HEAVEN SEAL **1** GOLDEN DEITY	BIG AUSPICIOUS **3** BIG AUSPICIOUS	YEARLY CONFLICT **8** YI DUO STAR
NE	NORTH	NW

EAST — WEST

The chart for 2011 indicates different numbers in each of the nine grids in this three by three sector chart. This looks like the original Lo Su square which plays such a big role in time dimension feng shui except that each year, the numbers placed in each grid change according to the center number. With 7 in the center, the other numbers are then placed around the grid sectors. This is what changes the pattern of energy in homes and offices from year to year.

The numbers play a big part in determining the "*luck outlook*" of animal signs arising from the fact that each of the twelve signs occupies a designated compass location. Thus the Snake person occupies the Southeast location and we can see from the chart that the Snake sign is influenced by the lucky number 6 which brings financial and other windfalls. The year will surprise you with some positive development.

The Snake is flanked by two beneficial stars - *Big Auspicious star* on one side and *Small Auspicious star* on the other. These are the stars of the 24 Mountains and they are indicative of auspicious developments happening in 2011. The Snake also sits on the star of the Small Auspicious which brings yet more good fortune.

The stars of the 24 mountains are very influential. There are 108 different fortune stars but only a handful fly into the 24 directions in any year. These bring auspicious or harmful influences, but they vary in strength and type each year. Houses and animal signs are affected in similar measure by these 24 mountain stars. Some stars bring good luck and protection while some bring misfortune. To activate them it is good to wear enhancing amulets.

We have made several enhancing amulets that are suitable for the Snake sign. These are highlighted in Section 7 of the book.

Houses and animal signs are affected in similar measure by the 24 mountain stars. Some stars bring good luck, some bring misfortune, while others bring protection. When your sign is negatively afflicted and your vitality gets weakened, you need to wear specific protective Taoist charms to remedy afflictions and activate good indications.

The Annual Protection Amulet has been specially designed to protect against specific afflictions in the year 2011.

Staying Updated Each Month

In many ways, the monthly updates are the highlight of this book; good timing plays an important part in actualizing good fortune and in avoiding misfortunes. To enjoy good luck during the year, you must update your feng shui. Hence, you need to know how cosmic energies affect your luck every month.

Every animal sign can be alerted to the high and low points of their year, and be warned against negative energy, as well as to spur you on during months when your chi energy is high. When to lie low and when to be go bravely forth are important to maximizing the opportunities of the year, so irrespective of whether the year is good or bad, you can avoid pitfalls and avoid missing out on opportunities that come your way.

Nothing beats being prepared against potential misfortune because this reduces their impact. Knowing the nature of misfortune - whether it is related to illness or accident, betrayal or plain bad luck - helps you cope when the misfortune does occur. What is better is that when you wear protective remedies, mantra amulets or talismans, these are very effective in warding off misfortune.

Thus an important aspect of reading these books is to take note of the spikes and dips in your monthly luck focusing on Career, Business, Family, Love and Study luck. The monthly readings analyze each month's Lo Shu numbers, element, trigram and paht chee luck pillars. These accurately identify your good and bad months; they generate valuable pointers on how to navigate safely and successfully through the year, effectively helping you get your timing right on important decisions and actions.

The recommendations in this book alert you to months when you are vulnerable to illness, accidents or dangers. We also highlight good luck months and this is when exciting new opportunities come to you. Knowing when will give you a competitive edge on timing. You will get better at coping with setbacks and overcoming obstacles that occur from month to month.

Improving Your Luck

Your luck can also be substantially improved through the placement of symbolic enhancers or remedies to the space you occupy. This is a book on the personalized approach for you to attract good luck. You will see as you delve deeper into it that there are many ways you can improve your personalized luck.

What is needed in each of the compass sectors of your home changes from year to year. In 2011 what the Snake sign needs for the Southeast location is to energize the power of 6 with six rod wind chime made of metal. This will generate the chi that activates the 6 star. It is also beneficial to place water in the SE sector of your garden.

For those of you wanting to get seriously wealthy, you might want to consider building a large waterfall in the SE of your garden (if you have the space to do so). This is what can really bring you the BIG luck opportunities. Make your waterfall as large as you can afford and as big as your home will allow you to. Those who lack the space it is unfortunate but you simply do not have the karma yet to become seriously wealthy. But a small **water feature** in the SE will nevertheless attract some new money!

Activate money luck this year with a **water feature** in the Southeast.

How you react to the year's changing energies depend on the strength of your spirit essence and your life force. This year 2011 however both of these important indications stay the same as last year. There is no change to your life force and spiritual strength, so the Snake sign continues to experience good strength in these two areas. Only the success potential has changed. This section of the book has thus been considerably shortened. In its place, we are introducing a new aspect that affect your fortunes.

The extra dimension we address this year is to introduce you to your SKY ANIMAL sign. In addition to one's year of birth animal sign, destiny and attitudes are also influenced by one's lunar mansion.

This is represented by one of the 28 sky animals that correspond to the 28 days in a typical month. This is your Day Sign and it interacts with your Year Sign to add important new dimensions to your compatibility with others, and to your luck outlook each year.

Your Lunar Mansion

This is based on the four great constellations that are the foundation of feng shui - the constellations of the *Green Dragon, Crimson Phoenix, Black Tortoise* and *White Tiger*. The **Green Dragon** rules the Eastern skies, while the **Crimson Phoenix** rules the Southern skies. The **White Tiger** is Lord of the Western Skies and the **Black Tortoise** oversees the Northern skies. Collectively, they rule over the 28 Sky Animals each having dominance over 7 of them. Depending on which of the 28 animals is your Day sign, you are under the influence of (and thus protected by) the Dragon, Tiger, the Phoenix or the Tortoise. These are termed the constellations of the lunar mansion.

Your Sky Animal brings additional insights to the kind of luck you enjoy in any given year depending on

your profession or business. The year 2011 is ruled by the Eastern sign of the Rabbit; and with two Tigers in the Pillars chart, this is a year when the Green Dragon who rules the Eastern Skies is dominant.

Those whose Day Sign comes under the mighty Dragon are more likely to benefit from the Dragon. Thus bringing the image of the Dragon into your home would be excellent for everyone, but especially so for you, as you are born in the year of the Dragon. The Dragon image was very beneficial last year and continues to be the celestial creature that brings good fortune to the year 2011. And since the Water element continues to be in short supply, it is as beneficial to have water and Dragon together, especially in the East of your home where it enhances the Rabbit Year, working with the Tiger presence in the Pillars chart to create the Zodiac trinity combination of Spring.

The wearing of any kind of crystal or crystal embossed with **Dragon** or any kind of **Dragon jewellery** is especially beneficial in 2011. You also benefit from wearing big chunky natural quartz crystals in 2011 as this signifies the grounding Earth element that is missing from the Pillars chart.

Earth is what provides the year's resources. It strengthens the intrinsic element of the Dragon to balance the double Tiger hence transforming the year's Tiger energy to work powerfully in your favor. It also combines with the Tiger to strengthen the Rabbit energy of the year. This helps to defuse the ferocity of the clashing elements at an individualized level.

Determining your lunar mansion Day Animal requires access to specific calculations retrieved from the Chinese Almanac. In this book, these calculations have been simplified, and any one can quite easily work out their Day Animal sign from the chapter on your lunar mansion. These offer additional insights into your luck outlook for the year.

Updating Your Feng Shui

Buildings are affected by new energy patterns each year, so knowing how to work with these new energies is what unlocks good fortune each year. It is thus important to focus attention on the remedial updates required to safeguard the feng shui of your home and office. This aspect of feng shui is the time dimension of this living skill.

Because energy transforms at the start of the year, changing as it does on the day of Spring popularly referred to as the day of the *lap chun*, it is thus vital that all updates should be done before this date which falls on February 4th, 2011. This also corresponds to the start of the solar year of the *Chinese Hsia calendar*. Remedial cures are always necessary to subdue the effects of negative stars and malicious influences of bad luck numbers in the flying star chart. The location and strength of these negative influences change from year to year and feng shui practitioners suppress their influence to reduce the incidence of misfortune luck, accidents, illness and other afflictions.

Three Dimensions in Feng Shui

Feng shui has three dimensions to its practice, a space, time and self-empowering dimension. These address the heaven, earth and mankind chi that make up the trinity of luck that collectively account for how luck works for or against us. If you want to benefit from total feng shui, you should use the collective power of all three dimensions.

Space dimension is governed by environmental feng shui methods - collectively practiced under the broad umbrella of what everyone terms feng shui. Here, it comprises the art of living in harmony with natural landforms and the art of placing auspicious objects with great symbolic meaning and element properties around us. Environmental feng shui takes note of compass directions on a personalized basis and use other methods that focus on lucky and unlucky sectors. Broadly speaking, it takes care of the Earth aspect in the trinity of luck.

Then there is *time dimension feng shui*, which requires our practice to take note of changing and transformational energies. These indicate that energy is never still; that it is constantly changing, and it is therefore necessary to always take cognizance of how energy transforms over various overlapping cycles of time; annually, monthly, daily, hourly and even in larger time frames that last 20 years, 60 years and even 180 years, which is the time it takes for a full nine period cycle of 20 years to complete.

Here in this book, we focus very much on the all-important annual cycles of change, but we also look at the monthly cycles; and we write this book on the basis that we are living through the larger cycle of the Period of 8. Broadly speaking, time feng shui takes care of the HEAVENLY cosmic forces that affect the overall trinity of luck.

Finally, there is the self or spiritual dimension, which broadly speaking depends on the energies generated by MANKIND. This focuses on the chi energy individually as well as collectively created or produced by people themselves. How we each individually, and together with others who live with us, empower the energy of self to either create good or bad energy.

In its highest form, the Self energy is believed to be the most powerful of all, and in the face even of extremely challenging **Heaven Luck** as is the case in 2011, the highly empowered self or highly focused person who has the ability to use the powerful forces of his/her mental concentration can indeed generate the all-powerful **Mankind** chi that can subdue afflictions brought by the intangible conflicting energy of the year's forces (**Heaven Luck**) as well as tangible bad energy caused by bad feng shui (**Earth Luck**).

The highly empowered self does not just happen. This too requires learning, practice and experience, and it involves developing a highly focused and concentrated mind that can generate powerful chi. This is spiritual chi that takes years to develop, but there are methods - both gross and subtle - that can be used to generate good mankind luck.

These methods are referred to as *inner feng shui*. Traditonal feng shui masters of the old school are great adepts at invoking the Taoist spiritual deities through meditative contemplations and meditations, reciting powerful prayers and mantras and using powerful purification rituals to remove obstacles.

Many turn to Buddhist deities who are believed to be very powerful in helping to awaken the inner forces within us. A great deal of feng shui history is thus tied up with Taoism and Buddhist practices in ancient China. However, this aspect of feng shui is usually kept secret by the Masters, many of whom are also expert at meditation and visualization techniques. It is their meditations that enable them to access their highly empowered inner chi which brings their practice of feng shui to a much higher level of accomplishment.

We found out that many of the powerful ancient rituals for overcoming life obstacles such as those using incense and aromas and the empowerment of symbolic and holy objects to enhance the spiritual feng shui of homes found their way to Tibet during the Tang dynasty, where they were incorporated into their spiritual practices, especially those practices that invoked the powerful Protectors of the Land of

Snows. These powerful rituals are now being revealed to the world by the high lamas of Tibetan Buddhism.

In 2011, it will be especially effective in practicing this method of feng shui, as it will alleviate many of the discordant energies of the coming year.

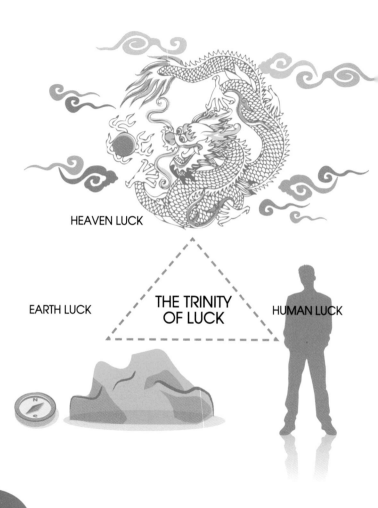

HEAVEN LUCK

THE TRINITY
OF LUCK

EARTH LUCK

HUMAN LUCK

Snake Enjoys a Surge of Good Fortune in 2011

- Metal Snake – 10 & 70 years
- Water Snake – 58 years
- Wood Snake – 46 years
- Fire Snake – 34 years
- Earth Snake – 22 years

Outlook for the Snake In 2011

Those born in the year of the Snake can look forward to another great year. In 2011, the Snake has fewer worries than the previous year and all indications of feng shui winds and cosmic forces influencing your year are positive. Combined with your strong life force and spirit essence, this means that you enjoy auspicious luck, and more importantly, you will be strong enough to receive the good fortune. Whatever you set your mind on doing, you are certain to achieve in full measure.

The Snake horoscope chart registers triple OOOs in Life Force luck and Spiritual Essence luck, which means that not only do you enjoy good luck, you are also very blessed and protected. Since this is the second year running that you are enjoying these indications, do try to make the most of it so you do not waste the year. Put new plans and strategies into motion to grow and to expand.

> In 2011 you are on a roll and you must strike when there is such intensity of good fortune helping you. Good years rarely come bunched together the way it has for the Snake this year.

You benefit from the number 6 star as this creates an excellent flow of feng shui winds coming your way. The number 6 is a heavenly star which brings all the goodness of the Chien trigram of the Northwest; and this year, the NW direction which houses this trigram and which lies opposite to the Snake's SE is visited by the number 8 star. The two numbers 8 and 6 are white numbers, so there is awesome compatibility of numbers here. This benefits all the animal signs in the two directions of SE (the Snake and the Dragon) and NW (the Dog and the Boar). For the Snake, the configuration of these auspicious stars is quite awesome because you also have some powerful 24 mountain stars helping you. You have the ability to generate new strategies that help leapfrog you into a different league. Yes, you have the success touch this year so make things happen!

The Water and Fire Snakes especially should be strongly motivated to think big and aim high. Parlay a whole series of small successes into new directions that bring the potential to make it big in the coming years. Build your foundation strongly and firmly.

The Snake Personality in 2011

The Snake gains in confidence and self-assurance in 2011. Buoyed by the successes of the previous year - in whatever endeavour you may have been pursuing - whether in business or in sports, in academia or in professional working life - you have experienced the high of achievement last year. The good news is that for you, this new year 2011 continues to be as positively eventful. There is more coming your way and it is likely that you can and will build on the successes of last year. You are transforming from a humble green snake into a magnificent python or cobra, a winner in more ways than you can imagine. So there will be a renewed air of self assurance to your personality. This may or may not be a good thing, as it can come out negative or positive.

For some of you, the success of the past year might make you more arrogant, even big headed, and if so, you run the risk of coming across quite unbearable. You might then turn off quite a lot of admirers! So while it is acceptable to take pride in what you have accomplished, it is as important to stay humble. There is still a great deal to do and it is not smart to spoil your chances of attaining greater success this year by becoming too big for your shoes. Remember that pride does come before a fall!

For others, the attainment of highs could transform you into an irresistible and charming personality; there is nothing more attractive than a successful person who is humble and un aggressive. If the realization of your goals makes you more aware than ever of the heights of mountains, you are sure to keep climbing higher and higher.

Happily, the Snake personality has always been laced with a veneer of the seductive. Many people find the Snake sign very appealing. The Fire and Earth Snakes will likely transform from the young innocent to the wise old thing and for the others, there is definitely a transformation taking place in your Snake personality. The Snake gains in wisdom from year to year. In good years they do tend to become less judgemental of others and more tolerant of other viewpoints.

New found assurance and wisdom is sure to boost their standing amongst their peers, thus steering them to higher levels and even to a new league. This is especially true of Snakes in their thirties and forties. Those in their forties and fifties will be in less awe of the renewed progress taking place in their lives as they are more experienced and pragmatic.

OUTLOOK FOR
THE LADY SNAKE IN 2011

BIRTH YEAR	TYPE OF SNAKE LADY	LO SHU AT BIRTH	AGE	LUCK OUTLOOK IN 2011
1941	Metal Snake Lady	5	70	A strong year with financial shortfall
1953	Water Snake Lady	2	58	Exceptionally great year financially
1965	Wood Snake Lady	8	46	Everything good but money is short
1977	Fire Snake Lady	5	34	Everything going great, watch health
1989	Earth Snake Lady	2	22	A good year with good success luck
2001	Metal Snake Girl	8	10	Strong year but watch your purse

In the year 2011, the Lady Snake comes out of her shell and becomes extra active socially, going out more and enlarging her group of friends. This is a year when work mixes seamlessly with your social life and your hobbies. There will be few money or health problems for you, so you practically have a blank canvas to paint on it the kind of year you want. Only Fire and Earth Snakes need to be careful not to expose themselves to health risks. All others are in good shape. Money-wise, the charts indicate that there are no blockages to the

Part 2 : Snake Enjoys a Surge of Good Fortune in 2011

continuous flow of income coming your way; and there could even be more, depending on what you get up to.

Ladies born under the Snake sign are smart in their dealings in business. They understand strategy and they appreciate clarity of thinking. But they are also very feminine, appearing non-threatening while being completely on top of things. In short, the Snake woman is a formidable adversary simply because it is so rare to see a Snake woman with bared fangs. They come across soft spoken and reveal little of what goes on inside their pretty heads.

The Snake lady is very aware that her life is opening new horizons for her to conquer. Some of the key decisions she made in the recent past years have turned out well, thereby giving her a new poise and self assurance. She possess hidden strength and her inner energy continues to be stable and robust. What is exciting is her renewed sense of purpose. In 2011 she will be more focused than ever; and it is this determination that can and probably will propel her into a different league.

Snake women possess an independent spirit that but are not stubborn. They are no pushovers as those who try to take advantage of them will find out very quickly. These ladies also have a very special skill in the way they make their entrances and exits - usually quietly and without too much fuss. Sometimes they are so understated and so low key, you hardly notice them in a roomful of people. But herein lies their great strength - they can be unobtrusive, yet can effortlessly generate a great performance.

Snake women are persuasive without being offensive. In 2011, they have the added advantage of having a powerful aura and a strong spiritual presence. This, with the good influences indicated in the year's chart, bring good winds blowing their way.

OUTLOOK FOR THE GENTLEMAN SNAKE IN 2011

BIRTH YEAR	TYPE OF SNAKE MAN	LO SHU AT BIRTH	AGE	LUCK OUTLOOK IN 2011
1941	Metal Snake Man	6	70	Good year to take things easy
1953	Water Snake Man	3	58	Enjoying a second wind this year
1965	Wood Snake Man	9	46	Romance luck bring temptations
1977	Fire Snake Man	6	34	Wonderful financial luck
1989	Earth Snake Man	3	22	Career and work place stressful
2001	Metal Snake Boy	9	10	Good to stay focused on exams

The gentleman Snake can also look forward to a strong and robust year. For many of you, 2011 can become a benchmark year, especially if you can seamlessly build on what you set up last year. The past year was exceptionally good for the Snake man as well and this can be seen as the follow up year - the sequel so to speak. In terms of outlook therefore, you have many good things to look forward to. For some, success comes with great financial gains as well and this is especially true for the 59 year old **Water Snake** gentleman. All signs point to a strong year for the Snake Patriarch, and especially with the indications for patriarchal luck in 2011 at such an all-time high. Note that the number 8 in the feng shi chart has flown to the Northwest, which is where the luck of the patriarch resides. With the 8 comes excellent luck and with the NW being directly opposite the Snake's SE location, the indications are favorable for male Snakes, especially those of you who are leaders, or are fathers or are heading a company or a department in your organization. The number 8 is also highly compatible with your number that is influencing the Snake this year which is 6. Both are white numbers and are auspicious.

The number 6 also brings heaven luck and this resonates strongly with the chien trigram of the Northwest. These associations benefit the Snake gentleman more than their female counterparts but mainly to those of you who can qualify for the term patriarch.

If you are a male Snake and you are single, your luck is also very good this year but it is nowhere as strong. You have natural protection arising from strong life force in your element horoscope; your inner spiritual strength is also vigorous so there is little that can stand in your way. But the energies that are supporting you are good and pure energies and it is important that those of you who are still young should follow the wise counsel of older people around you. In 2011 the gentleman Snake must refrain from being arrogant or imperious.

You have an exciting and favorable year ahead. There is continuous occurrence of good fortune coming. Do not take it for granted otherwise blockages to your luck start to manifest.

Moving into a Bigger League in 2011

The Snake's personal horoscope luck in 2011 suggests success continues to be strong although in terms of last year's indication there is a marginal drop from OOO to OO. However, this year the Snake is helped by other more powerfully auspicious indications and it is likely that for you, the good luck of the previous year continues seamlessly into this year. The coming twelve months should be strong and robust with business and professional goals being met easily.

The successes of the previous year should be easy to maintain and improved upon. The Snake should be feeling blessed in 2011 as you can quite easily sail through the year. There are few afflictions to contend with and whatever may cause you anguish brought by monthly stars should not be difficult to handle.

The Snake will find that professionally, and in business, things move smoothly and they can set their own pace as to how and what they want from the year. You can be as ambitious as you wish. You also have a strong elemental horoscope chart this year so you are in a good position to define your own boundaries.

Usually however, whenever a sign enjoys a powerful Life Force and this is matched by an equally strong spiritual presence, then even without doing anything; good fortune brings good things your way. This is the power of fate, of destiny. When the time is right, that is when things happen through the ripening of good fortune. Some call this the harvesting of good past karma. Call it what you wish!

But you can get ready to move to a new and higher league. It is that kind of year for you, and long after you finish reading this and have forgotten, just remember to rejoice when good fortune does come your way; even if you are not terribly ambitious, when good things come your way, accept them graciously.

Personal Horoscope Luck in 2011

The horoscope chart of elements for each Snake is determined by the heavenly stem element of your year of birth. It shows how the Snake's ruling luck Elements in its year of birth interacts with the luck Elements of the year 2011. This interaction reveals whether five types of luck are good or bad each year. When the elements governing the five kinds of luck for each sign interact badly with the equivalent elements of 2011 it means the luck is bad. When it interacts positively it means that luck is good.

For the Snake, your Life Force is showing a triple OOO, which is superlative; All Snakes benefit from this indication of their birth elements interacting with the elements of the year. It indicates that overall luck continues to be strong and that the year's energy protects you, guarding your good fortune and preventing bad luck from hurting you.

Anyone trying to harm you will find it rebounds back to them, so bad people canot come near you. The Chinese respect this energy and refer to it as a magical aura of protection. It is like having a guardian angel watching over you. All Snake sign people enjoy this protective power in 2011.

Meanwhile, the Snake's Spirit Essence continues to be at a very high level in 2011 as well; registering a reading of triple OOO. Circles always suggest natural protection against spiritual harm and other afflictions. The three OOOs is an indication of holy beings watching over you.

This is a very lucky and auspicious meaning. You are not just spiritually safe but also shielded against poor health, loss of wealth or obstacles that hinder your success luck. So the triple OOOs not only protect, they also imply that there is a powerful aura around you.

Another thing: usually when the Spirit Essence is strong in any year, you will find yourself being very good at empowering the mind; you can practice spiritual feng shui because your inner essence is strong and can be used to manifest what you want into auspicious reality.

It is worthwhile learning some powerful meditation techniques that include visualisation methods as well. To not do so would be a real waste as receiving such powerful indications of internal strength is does not happen often.

Metal Snake - 70 or 10 Years Old

TYPE OF LUCK	ELEMENT AT BIRTH AFFECTING THIS LUCK	ELEMENT IN 2011 AFFECTING THIS LUCK	LUCK RATING
LIFE FORCE	Fire	Wood	OOO
HEALTH LUCK	Metal	Wood	OO
FINANCE LUCK	Metal	Metal	X
SUCCESS LUCK	Water	Fire	OO
SPIRIT ESSENCE	Wood	Water	OOO

HEALTH LUCK - showing OO indicates good health for the year with no problems.

FINANCE LUCK - showing X indicates no noticeable increase in wealth this year, perhaps even a small loss.

SUCCESS LUCK - showing OO, a marginal decrease over last year, but still strong in view of other readings.

Water Snake - 58 Years Old

TYPE OF LUCK	ELEMENT AT BIRTH AFFECTING THIS LUCK	ELEMENT IN 2011 AFFECTING THIS LUCK	LUCK RATING
LIFE FORCE	Fire	Wood	XX
HEALTH LUCK	Water	Wood	OX
FINANCE LUCK	Water	Metal	OOO
SUCCESS LUCK	Water	Fire	OX
SPIRIT ESSENCE	Wood	Water	XX

HEALTH LUCK - showing OX suggests good health because the O overcomes the X here.

FINANCE LUCK - showing OOO means your financial situation will show a noticeable improvement.

SUCCESS LUCK - showing OO a marginal decrease over last year, but still strong in view of other readings.

Wood Snake - 46 Years Old

TYPE OF LUCK	ELEMENT AT BIRTH AFFECTING THIS LUCK	ELEMENT IN 2011 AFFECTING THIS LUCK	LUCK RATING
LIFE FORCE	Fire	Wood	OOO
HEALTH LUCK	Fire	Wood	OOO
FINANCE LUCK	Wood	Metal	XX
SUCCESS LUCK	Water	Fire	OO
SPIRIT ESSENCE	Wood	Water	OOO

HEALTH LUCK - showing OOO suggests that physically you are strong and very healthy. No problems..

FINANCE LUCK - showing XX means you need to be very careful with your finances. You could sustain a loss.

SUCCESS LUCK - showing OO. A marginal decrease over last year, but still strong in view of other readings.

Fire Snake - 34 Years Old

TYPE OF LUCK	ELEMENT AT BIRTH AFFECTING THIS LUCK	ELEMENT IN 2011 AFFECTING THIS LUCK	LUCK RATING
LIFE FORCE	Fire	Wood	OOO
HEALTH LUCK	Earth	Wood	XX
FINANCE LUCK	Fire	Metal	OO
SUCCESS LUCK	Water	Fire	OO
SPIRIT ESSENCE	Wood	Water	OOO

HEALTH LUCK - showing XX indicates some kind of health ailment could befall you.

FINANCE LUCK - showing OO means financial luck is sure to improve in 2011. Good indication.

SUCCESS LUCK - showing OO. A marginal decrease over last year but still strong in view of other readings.

Earth Snake - 22 Years Old

TYPE OF LUCK	ELEMENT AT BIRTH AFFECTING THIS LUCK	ELEMENT IN 2011 AFFECTING THIS LUCK	LUCK RATING
LIFE FORCE	Fire	Wood	000
HEALTH LUCK	Wood	Wood	X
FINANCE LUCK	Earth	Metal	OX
SUCCESS LUCK	Water	Fire	00
SPIRIT ESSENCE	Wood	Water	000

HEALTH LUCK - showing X suggests minor health related ailments this year.

FINANCE LUCK - showing OX indicates stability of finances but it is still good to be careful.

SUCCESS LUCK - showing OO. A marginal decrease over last year but still very good. Be discerning!

Discovering Your Lunar Mansion

Part 3

How Your Sky Animal Affects Your Luck

Your lunar mansion is named one of 28 Sky animals that pinpoint the Day of the week that is favorable for you and more importantly it reveals what sky constellation you belong to, thereby opening up a mine of information as to the kind of people you work best with; the area of work that offers the best potential for success; and the nature of the assistance your Sky Animal brings you in any given year. Your Lunar Mansion is an integral part of you, so it deepens your understanding of what makes you tick, how it modifies the attitude tendencies and the outlook for your Zodiac sign.

DISCOVERING YOUR LUNAR MANSION

How Your Sky Animal Affects Your Luck

There are four Sky constellations under each of which are seven Sky Animals, three of them primary and four, secondary. Those of you born in a Snake Year will work well with Sky Animals belonging to the Southern Skies and as a team or partnership they attract good business luck. At the same time, your own Sky Animal will likewise determine which of other Sky Animals work well with you. Basically, these are colleagues belonging to the same constellation as you.

Each constellation refers to one of four sections of the Skies, which are associated with the Four Celestial Guardians, the **Green Dragon**, who guards the Eastern skies, the **Crimson Phoenix** protects the Southern Skies, the **Black Tortoise** lord of the Northern Skies and the **White Tiger** who rules the Western Skies. The Celestials and the Sky Animals mirror the Celestial Guardians of feng shui, and the Zodiac animal signs that make up the earthly branches of Astrology. This mirror effect strengthens specific types of good fortune. Sky Animals rarely bring obstacles as their effect is generally positive. They signify the influence of heaven.

Lucky Day

Everyone is born on a DAY that corresponds to one of these Sky Animals. In astrological terms, this is the lucky DAY for you. It is described as your corresponding lunar mansion and it reveals the influence of star constellations on your professional and business life from year to year. One's lunar mansion is analyzed in conjunction with one's personal Four pillars chart and the Four Pillars chart of the year. Such a detailed analysis is not within the scope of this book, but it is useful to know the trends brought by the influence of your lunar mansion (or Sky Animal) in terms of your relationships and your luck in 2011.

Compatibility

For instance, everyone belonging to the same constellation and coming under the same Celestial Guardian has an affinity with each other, and in times of trouble, one can depend on the other, sometimes even in spite of them being opposing signs based on year of birth.

Sky animals also have natural affinity to their corresponding Zodiac animal signs e.g. a Sky Snake has affinity with someone born in the year of the Snake and vice versa and Sky Snake and also have affinity with someone born in the year of the Rooster or Ox (Snake's allies). This applies for all 12 animal Zodiac signs as each sign has a Sky counterpart!

Meanwhile, you can also be a secret friend of a Sky animal. Thus the Sky Monkey is the secret friend of the Snake. This creates very powerful work luck as your heaven and earth chi blend well. This is a heaven and earth relationship. In itself, this is an indication of auspicious chi, so it is good for the Snake to go into partnership with someone who is a Sky Monkey.

Determining the Dominant Celestial Guardian

The coming year 2011 is a Rabbit Year with two Tigers and a Horse in its Pillars chart. This suggests that the Green Dragon who rules the Eastern Skies is dominant. This arises from it being a Rabbit Year and the Rabbit is one of the Sky signs belonging to the Dragon constellation.

The Dragon rules the Skies of the East and included in this constellation are also the Sky Tiger. The Zodiac Tiger whose location is part of the East also makes appearances in the year's paht chee. The strength and influence of the Dragon's constellation is thus very powerful in 2011. It is definitely beneficial to invite the image of the Dragon into the home in 2011.

Note especially that in 2011, the lunar year begins on the **3rd of February** which corresponds to the day before the lap chun, the day of Spring. This is an auspicious indication. This could bring miracles to the year and help in transforming conflict energy into something productive.

With the Dragon as the ruling celestial guardian, growth energy during the year will be strong. The Sky Dragon is the key to subduing all discordant energies brought by the clashing elements on earth. Lining up all seven animals of the Dragon's constellation is believed to bring greater strength for getting projects started and attracting the good fortune of the Sky Dragon constellation. This applies to the Rabbit, its seasonal ally, the Dragon, as well as to those born in the sign of the Tiger.

Even just placing the three main Sky signs of this constellation - the Dragon, Tiger and Rabbit - would be extremely auspicious and it benefits to place them in the East part of your garden or along an East wall of your living room. Sky signs look exactly like their Zodiac counterparts.

Green Dragon Constellation

The seven Sky Animals that belong to the Dragon's constellation of the Eastern skies are the Sky Dragon, Sky Rabbit and Sky Tiger, as well as the Sky Salamander, Beaver, Fox and Leopard.

1. The Sky Salamander

This sky creature epitomizes the phenomenon of growth energy, associated mainly with agriculture and plantations. Any kind of profession associated with plants, gardens or plantations would be beneficial. This creature is a cousin of the Dragon but it is also close to the Snake so if this is your Lunar Mansion, your creative instincts should be strong. You have good fortune in 2011 and your heaven luck is good. Your lucky day is Thursday.

2. The Sky Dragon

This powerful creature is said to be a magician, able to create wondrous things out of nothing more than dreams. Success comes early in life and you could peak earlier than you wish; the Snake born with this sign can literally create magic, finding strength in pursuing its own ideas and operating with high confidence. You can take some risks this year and there could be big things coming your way in 2011. Stay relaxed! Your lucky day is Friday.

3. The Sky Beaver

This is a creature that signifies stability and good foundation. If this is your sign, you should seek out mentors, people senior to you who could bring you *"follow my leader luck"*. A Snake born with this Sky Animal sign usually benefits enormously because the Sky Beaver enhances your networking luck which will open pathways to many lucrative opportunities. Your lucky day is Saturday.

4. The Sky Rabbit

This is the most accommodating creature of this Constellation, usually associated with bringing family members together and establishing the bliss of domestic

comforts. A Snake born with this sign will put family above work in 2011. Your lucky day is Sunday.

5. The Sky Fox

This crafty, alert and quick-witted creature blends with the character of the ambitious Snake personality. Described as the heart and soul

of the Dragon constellation, this creature can steer you to a high position and great success. An asset to any of the twelve signs of the Zodiac. Your lucky day is Monday.

6. The Sky Tiger

This is the creature is said to be born with a jade pendant on its forehead; so power and authority comes naturally to anyone who is a Sky Tiger. Success can be assured in the political arena and they also receive unexpected windfalls of luck all through their life, attracting help and support from family and friends. This Lunar Mansion blends with the Snake born, bringing you some auspicious luck in 2011. Your lucky day is Tuesday.

7. The Sky Leopard

This is the creature that benefits from being close to the Dragon; the wind beneath the sails, the faithful second in command. Sky leopards are almost always surrounded by many of the good things in life whether or not these belong to them. Nevertheless they are able to enjoy life's luxuries. The Snake born as a Sky Leopard can achieve great success if they are discreet, loyal and keep their own counsel. Your lucky day is Wednesday.

Black Tortoise Constellation

For the Snake born, if your Sky Animal comes under the Tortoise constellation, you personify the good life with little effort. This creates energies that make it easy for you to take fullest advantage of your good fortune indications in 2011. It becomes a double bonus this year. The animals of the Tortoise Constellation are the Sky Ox (NE1), the Sky Rat (North), and the Sky Boar (NW3). There are also the Sky Unicorn, the Sky Bat, the Sky Swallow and the Sky Porcupine.

8. The Sky Unicorn

This creature combines the speed of the Horse with the courage of the Dragon. For the Snake, if this is your Sky Animal, it indicates two extreme sides of you, for the Unicorn is at once your best friend and your own worst enemy. Snake born people whose Sky counterpart is the Unicorn could have an exaggerated sense of do goodness about them. You have to look beyond small grievances and take the big picture approach to attaining all your dreams. Make sure you do not lose out on the main chance. Your lucky day is Thursday.

9. The Sky Ox

This creature is associated with the legend of the weaving maiden and the Ox boy forced to live apart and able to meet only once a year. Snake born people whose Sky animal is the Ox will be especially strong as Ox is its ally so there is extremely favorable luck in 2011, especially in real estate investments. The single Snake could also find true love this year but there might be small obstacles. Your lucky day is Friday.

10. The Sky Bat

This is a secondary sign of the Tortoise constellation but it is a symbol that signifies extreme good fortune.

Benefits keep coming to you, especially if you are in the construction or engineering profession. Snake people with this Sky sign enjoy a life of comfort, living in a mansion through adult life. The Bat is greatly blessed if living in a temple or turns spiritual. There is good fortune awaiting you in 2011. Your lucky day is Saturday.

11. The Sky Rat

This sign signifies winter where yin energy rules. The Snake whose Sky sign is the Sky Rat enjoys auspicious luck brought by 2011. A very auspicious year awaits you. You will be on the receiving end of some good fortune. Your lucky day is Sunday.

12. The Sky Swallow

This is the sign often associated with foolhardiness and danger as the swallow flies too fast and too high. This is the risktaker of the Tortoise constellation and Snake born people having this Sky sign could be a little too impulsive, and as a result could rush into making ill-advised decisions. If this is your sign, it would be advantageous to reflect carefully before committing to anything new. Your lucky day is Monday.

13. The Sky Boar

This is a sign associated with the good life which gets better as you get older. Snake born having this Sky sign are sure to be living in a mansion. You will enjoy good fortune in 2011 and the older you are, the better the luck coming your way. Good year to move into a bigger house. Your lucky day is Tuesday.

14. The Sky Porcupine

This is the policeman of this constellation, always conscious of security, alert to people with dishonest intentions. Snake born people having this sign are artistic and hardworking; very committed to what they do. This is a year when you can excel; Do not lose confidence in yourself in 2011, otherwise you might not have the courage to accept what comes your way. Your lucky day is Wednesday.

White Tiger Constellation

The White Tiger constellation tends to be vulnerable in 2011, hence those born into this grouping are advised to take things easy and lie low. The Mountain stars affecting the Western skies are potentially disastrous, bringing misfortune. Taking risks could be dangerous and the year itself already shows several warning signs, so it is best not to be too adventurous or foolhardy.

Snake-born people whose Sky Animal falls under this constellation should be alert to warning signs; it is beneficial to take the conciliatory approach at all times. Also, discretion is the better part of valor and it is better to be safe than sorry. This is not a good year for these Sky Animals to be too adventurous. But being a Snake born, your year influence does not give you much protection this year.

The Tiger's constellation has the Sky Dog (NW1), the Sky Rooster (West) and the Sky Monkey (SW3). On a compass, you can see this reflects the Western skies sector. These are creatures of Autumn, when others are preparing to hibernate. In 2011, when the year is dangerous for this grouping of Sky Animals, it is a good time to stay less active.

The secondary Sky Animals of the Tiger Constellation - the Sky Wolf, Sky Pheasant, Sky Raven and Sky Ape - protect and support the main creatures with all seven coming under the care of the White Tiger. In astrological terms, the signs in the grouping of the Western Sky creatures are the most commercially-minded of all the Sky Animals. In 2011, protection is the keyword for those belonging to this constellation.

15. The Sky Wolf

This is an insecure creature with a tendency towards negativity, expecting the worse to happen. The Sky Wolf requires plenty of reassurance and it is this lack of confidence that is its worst drawback. A Snake who is a Sky Wolf must exert greater efforts to be upbeat especially in 2011. Confidence is the key to succeeding. Your lucky day is Thursday.

16. The Sky Dog

This is an excellent sky sign as it indicates a life of success. The Sky Dog always has a pile of treasures at its feet; commercial and business success comes easily and effortlessly and theirs is a life filled with celebration and merry making. The Snake who is also a Sky Dog can find success in 2011 benefiting from the stars of *Big Auspicious*. But you have conflicting emotions and you need to be careful this year. Your lucky day is Friday.

17. The Sky Pheasant

This is another extremely good Sky sign as the Pheasant indicates someone successful at creating and keeping their wealth. This is a Sky sign that is particularly suited to a career involving finance such as banking. This sign will also never be short of money as the Sky Pheasant attracts wealth continuously. Snake born people with this sign are sure to be rich, but should also be alert to anyone trying to con them of money! Your lucky day is Saturday.

18. The Sky Rooster

This creature reflects its Zodiac counterpart, being naturally vigilant and watchful. The Sky Rooster is described as the eyes and ears of the skies ever alert to those who would disturb the natural order. You are an excellent one to have around in 2011 which is a year when your instincts are at their most alert. Snake born with this Sky sign benefit from the ally relationship between it and the Rooster; you will be going through risky but potentially prosperous times. Your lucky day is Sunday.

19. The Sky Raven

This is the creature of the Sky that signifies extremely rich rewards from efforts expended. The Sky Raven is associated with success of the most outstanding kind. As long as you are determined enough, you will get what you work for. Snake born with this sign need to work hard to enjoy a fruitful year in 2011. Your lucky day is Monday.

20. The Sky Monkey

This is a natural born leader who assumes leadership responsibilities without hesitation, naturally extending protective arms outwards. They are thus charismatic and attractive. A Snake born with the sign of the Sky Monkey will be a role model of some kind. Others are inspired by you. Your lucky day is Tuesday.

21. The Sky Ape

This is the creature that signifies the important law of karma, ripening for them faster than for others. Thus the Sky Ape succeeds when they work and find life difficult when they slack off. Good deeds bring instant good rewards and likewise also vile deeds. A Snake with this Sky sign will have good instincts in 2011. Your lucky day is Wednesday.

Crimson Phoenix Constellation

The Crimson Phoenix rules the Southern skies and its Sky Animals are the Sky Horse (South), Sky Sheep (SW1), and Sky Snake (SE3). As with the creatures of the other constellations, any family or business entity represented by this group of Sky Animals under the Phoenix benefit each other immensely. Collectively they attract exciting opportunities; their best time comes during the summer months and working on weekends benefits them. The Sky Animals or lunar mansions of the Southern skies are:

22. The Sky Anteater

This is a creature that has the potential to exert great influence, but whether or not this can materialize depends on other factors. The Sky Anteater can be a catalyst, but it cannot initiate or spearhead a project or be a leader. But as someone supporting someone else, there is no better person. A Snake born with this Sky sign works well behind the scenes. Your lucky day is Thursday.

23. The Sky Sheep

This Sky sign indicates someone who will eventually become deeply spiritual or psychic. When developed to its fullest potential, such a person becomes incredibly charismatic - easily becoming an iconic source of inspiration to others. A Snake born with this Sky sign has the potential to achieve brilliance as industry leaders or politicians. Your lucky day is Friday.

24. The Sky Roebuck

This is a creature of healing, someone who has the gift to mend broken hearts and emotionally distraught people. Those with this Sky sign have calm dispositions, so a Snake born under this Sky sign will be an excellent calming influence on anyone. This sign usually do extremely well as counselors. Your lucky day is Saturday.

25. The Sky Horse

This is a lovely Sky sign loved by many people. Also referred to as the mediator of the skies, the Sky Horse takes everyone for a joyride, helping others forget their grievances with great effectiveness. A Snake born with this sign tends to be more adventurous than normal. Your lucky day is Sunday.

26. The Sky Deer

This is a generous creature whose spirit of giving endears it to many others. The Sky Deer is often also associated with those who make it to a high position and then using their influence and success to benefit many others. A Snake born with this Sky sign is sure to have this dimension of generosity in their personality. Your lucky day is Monday.

27. The Sky Snake

This creature represents imperial authority. The Sky Snake travels on the wings of the Phoenix, always ready to receive the applause and adoration of others. Sky Snakes enjoy the destiny of personal advancement, especially in the political arena. A Snake who is also a Sky Snake should watch for a good business opportunity in 2011. Your lucky day is Tuesday.

28. The Sky Worm

Humble as this creature may sound, the Sky Worm aims high, and when it succeeds, it does so with panache and great style. This is the great surprise of the constellation of lunar mansions because those born under this sign have great perseverance and amazing courage to take risks; success for them comes with a vengeance! The Snake with this sign should do well in 2011. Your lucky day is Wednesday.

Determining Your Sky Animal Sign

Example: If your day of birth is
25th October 1977

1. Get the corresponding number for your
   month and **year** from **Table 1**. Thus the
   number for October is 20, and the number
   for the year 1977 is 17.

2. Next, add the numbers of the month and
   the year to the day in October which is 25.
   Thus 20 + 17 + 25 = 62.

3. Next determine if your year of birth 1977 is
   a leap year; if it is, and you were born after
   March 1st add 1. Here 1977 is not a leap
   year, and you were born after March 1st, so
   here you do not add 1 to 62.

4. As 62 is more than 56, you need to subtract
   56 from 62. Thus 62 - 56 = 6. So note that
   for you, the Sky Animal is number 6.

To explain this part of the calculation note that since there are 28 animals, any number higher than 28 should deduct 28 and any number higher than 56 which is 28 x 2, should deduct 56 from the total to reach a number that is lower than 28. **This will indicate your Lunar Mansion number.**

Once you have your number, which in this example is 6, your Sky animal (or Lunar Mansion) is the one corresponding to the number 6 in Table 2 shown overleaf.

In this example of someone born on 25th October 1977, your Sky animal is the **Sky Tiger** and you belong to the Constellation of the **Green Dragon** of the Eastern skies. Your lucky day is **Monday** and you belong to the constellation season of **Spring**.

Meanwhile, based on your year of birth, you are born under the Zodiac sign of the **Fire Snake**.

TABLE 1
To Determine the Animal of Your Day of Birth

MONTH	YEAR	YEAR	YEAR	YEAR	YEAR	NO.
-	1920*	1942	-	1987	2009	1
FEB, MAR	-	1943	1965	1988*	2010	2
-	1921	1944*	1966	-	2011	3
-	1922	-	1967	1989	2012*	4
APRIL	1923	1945	1968*	1990		5
-	1924*	1946	-	1991	2013	6
MAY	-	1947	1969	1992*	2014	7
-	1925	1948*	1970	-	2015	8
-	1926	-	1971	1993	2016*	9
JUNE	1927	1949	1972*	1994		10
-	1928*	1950	-	1995	2017	11
JULY	-	1951	1973	1996*	2018	12
-	1929	1952*	1974	-	2019	13
-	1930	-	1975	1997	2020*	14
AUGUST	1931	1953	1976*	1998		15
-	1932*	1954	-	1999	2021	16
-	-	1955	1977	2000*	2022	17
SEPTEMBER	1933	1956*	1978	-	2023	18
-	1934	-	1979	2001	2024*	19
OCTOBER	1935	1957	1980*	2002		20
-	1936*	1958	-	2003	2025	21
-	-	1959	1981	2004*	2026	22
NOVEMBER	1937	1960*	1982	-	2027	23
-	1938	-	1983	2005	2028*	24
DECEMBER	1939	1961	1984*	2006	-	25
-	1940*	1962	-	2007	2029	26
JANUARY	-	1963	1985	2008*	2030	27
-	1941	1964*	1986	-	2031	28

* indicates a leap year

TABLE 2
The 28 Animals of the Four Constellations

**FAMILY OF THE GREEN DRAGON
RULING THE SEASON OF SPRING**

Lunar Mansion Constellations
of the **Eastern** skies

1. **Sky Salamander** THURSDAY
2. **Sky Dragon** FRIDAY
3. **Sky Beaver** SATURDAY
4. **Sky Rabbit** SUNDAY
5. **Sky Fox** MONDAY
6. **Sky Tiger** TUESDAY
7. **Sky Leopard** WEDNESDAY

**FAMILY OF THE BLACK TORTOISE
RULING THE SEASON OF WINTER**

Lunar Mansion Constellations
of the **Northern** skies

8. **Sky Unicorn** THURSDAY
9. **Sky Ox** FRIDAY
10. **Sky Bat** SATURDAY
11. **Sky Rat** SUNDAY
12. **Sky Swallow** MONDAY
13. **Sky Boar** TUESDAY
14. **Sky Porcupine** WEDNESDAY

**FAMILY OF THE WHITE TIGER
RULING THE SEASON OF AUTUMN**

Lunar Mansion Constellations
of the **Western** skies

15. **Sky Wolf** THURSDAY
16. **Sky Dog** FRIDAY
17. **Sky Pheasant** SATURDAY
18. **Sky Rooster** SUNDAY
19. **Sky Raven** MONDAY
20. **Sky Monkey** TUESDAY
21. **Sky Ape** WEDNESDAY

**FAMILY OF THE CRIMSON PHOENIX
RULING THE SEASON OF SUMMER**

Lunar Mansion Constellations
of the **Southern** skies

22. **Sky Ant Eater** THURSDAY
23. **Sky Sheep** FRIDAY
24. **Sky Antler** SATURDAY
25. **Sky Horse** SUNDAY
26. **Sky Deer** MONDAY
27. **Sky Snake** TUESDAY
28. **Sky Worm** WEDNESDAY

Interacting With Others In 2011

Part 4

Everyone Reacts Positively to Your Good Nature this Year

Many things affect how one animal sign gets along with another and the Chinese believe that much of this has to do with astrological forces and influences of a particular year. The varying factors result in a difference in compatibility levels each year and while it is impossible to take note of everything, the key variables to note are one's chi energy essence and whether the year's constellations are making you feel positive and good about yourself. The influence of the YEAR on the compatibilities of relationships is thus important; you cannot ignore the effect that annual chi has on the way you interact with your loved ones and family.

New energies influence the way you treat people, in turn determining how they respond to you. How you interact with close friends and loved ones is affected by your mental and physical state. So how you get on with your partner, your spouse, parents, children, siblings, relatives and friends are affected by your fortunes in any given year. But relationships are important because how these work out create important inputs to your happiness.

Understanding compatibility make you more understanding; when differences crop up, these need not be taken to heart. Good vibes make you tolerant while afflictive energies and negative stars suffered by others can make them seem tiresome.

Annual energy also influences what kind of people you will have greater or lesser affinity with. In some years you might feel an inexplicable aversion to someone you may always have liked and loved; or be attracted to someone you have always found annoying! Usually of course, the affinity groupings, secret friends alliances and ideal soul mate pairings of the Zodiac exert strong influences too, but annual chi plays a dominant role in swaying your thinking and those of others. They can make you more argumentative or make you more loving.

People tend to be more or less tolerant or selfish, cold or warm depending on the way things turn out for them from year to year. When life and work goes well, we become better disposed towards others. Then, even a natural zodiac enemy can become a soulmate, if only for a short period of time. Likewise, when one is being challenged by big problems, even the slightest provocation can lead to anger. Zodiac friends and allies might even then appear to be insufferable. A falling out between horoscope allies is thus not impossible.

In this section, we examine the Snake's personal relationships with the other eleven signs in 2011.

Zodiac Influences

1. Alliance of Allies
2. Zodiac Soulmates
3. Secret Friends
4. Astrology Enemies
5. Peach Blossom
6. Seasonal Trinity

1. Alliance of Allies

Four affinity groupings comprising three different animal signs form an alliance of natural allies in the Horoscope. These three signs share thought processes, aspirations and goals. Their attitudes are alike, and their support of each other is usually instinctive and long lasting. All three signs having good fortune in any year make the alliance strong and if there is an alliance within a family unit as amongst siblings, or between spouses and a child, the family is extremely supportive giving strength to each other. In good years, auspicious luck gets multiplied. Allies always get along. Any falling out is temporary. They trust each other and close ranks against external threats. Good astrological feng shui comes from carrying the image of your allies, especially when they are going through good years.

ALLY GROUPINGS	ANIMALS	CHARACTERISTICS
COMPETITORS	Rat, Dragon, Monkey	Competent, Tough, Resolute
INTELLECTUALS	Ox, Snake, Rooster	Generous, Focused, Resilient
ENTHUSIASTS	Dog, Tiger, Horse	Aggressive, Rebellious, Coy
DIPLOMATS	Boar, Sheep, Rabbit	Creative, Kind, Emotional

The Snake and its allies can establish a potentially lucrative alliance in 2011 as long as the afflictions affecting the Rooster can be contained. This ally's close encounter with the *Three Killings* and the *Tai Sui* can pose some problems, but with two of the three allies of this grouping enjoying strong Inner Essence and Life Force, the afflictions plaguing Rooster should not pose too big a problem. Both Snake and Ox fortunes suggest powerful prosperity opportunities, so as a team, Snake works well with Ox. Even with Rooster in a three party alliance, this group is strong because despite its afflictions, Rooster's feng shui winds bring the 9 star of future prosperity. So as long as the correct cures are put in place to deal with the year's afflictions this can become a potentially auspicious association.

The Snake, Rooster and Ox are Allies of the Chinese Zodiac.

Business associates that comprise the grouping of Snake, Ox and Rooster should do well in 2011. Of the three, it is you, the Snake, whose chi is strongest, with Rooster second and Ox having a negative rating in the Life Force and Inner Strength stakes. Despite this, you still benefit from the Ox person's victory vibes to enhance the Alliance. The Snake has excellent instincts in 2011, so do rely on your own judgments. In this alliance of intellectuals, you can be the leader. With your astrological allies, this can well turn out to be a benchmark year for you, especially with the 24 mountain stars bringing you some great new openings for development and the heavenly 6 star bringing good fortune possibilities.

2. Zodiac Soulmates

Six pairs of animal signs create six Zodiac Houses of yin and yang soul mates. Each pair creates powerful bonding at a cosmic level. Marriages or business unions between people belonging to the same Zodiac House are extremely auspicious. In a marriage, there is promise of great happiness. In a commercial partnership, it promises wealth and success. This pairing is good between professional colleagues and siblings. The strength of each pair is different; with

HOUSES OF PAIRED SOULMATES

ANIMALS	YIN/YANG	ZODIAC HOUSE OF CREATIVITY	TARGET UNLEASHED
Rat	YANG	HOUSE OF CREATIVITY & CLEVERNESS	The Rat initiates
Ox	YIN		The Ox completes
Tiger	YANG	HOUSE OF GROWTH & DEVELOPMENT	The Tiger employs force
Rabbit	YIN		The Rabbit uses diplomacy
Dragon	YANG	HOUSE OF MAGIC & SPRITITUALITY	The Dragon creates magic
Snake	YIN		The Snake creates mystery
Horse	YANG	HOUSE OF PASSION & SEXUALITY	The Horse embodies male energy
Sheep	YIN		The Sheep is the female energy
Monkey	YANG	HOUSE OF CAREER & COMMERCE	The Monkey creates strategy
Rooster	YIN		The Rooster get things moving
Dog	YANG	HOUSE OF DOMESTICITY	The Dog works to provide
Boar	YIN		The Boar enjoys what is created

their own defining strength, and with some making better commercial than marriage partners. How successful you are as a pair depends on how you bond. The table on the following page summarizes the key strength of each Zodiac house.

A coming together of yin Snake with its soulmate the yang Dragon creates the *House of Magic and Spirituality*. It is a strong alliance because these two are also regarded as celestial creatures, so their bond is strong and powerful, especially when they are together. In 2011, the Snake has strong Life Force and chi strength, and is stronger than the Dragon; so it is the Snake who will prevail. When these two animals get together in a business arrangement, benefits will accrue from the dynamism of the Dragon and the diplomatic skills of the Snake. So as a team, they create magic.

3. Secret Friends

There are six sets of a *secret friendship* that exists between the animal signs of the Zodiac. Between them a very powerful affinity exists making them excellent for each other. Love, respect and goodwill flow freely between secret friends; and they create wonderful happiness vibes for each other in a marriage. Once forged, it is a bond that is hard to break; and even when they themselves want to break, it will be hard for either party to fully walk away. This pair of signs will stick together through thick and thin. In the pairing of secret friends, the **Snake** is paired with the **Monkey**. There is a very special bond between these two signs. They are soulmates of the Zodiac, always there for each other irrespective of circumstance. Even when they may be bonded to others through marriage, still their attraction for one another can never be broken. A marriage between them will usually be extremely happy.

PAIRINGS OF SECRET FRIENDS

🐀	Rat	Ox	🐂
🐖	Boar	Tiger	🐅
🐕	Dog	Rabbit	🐇
🐉	Dragon	Rooster	🐓
🐍	Snake	Monkey	🐒
🐎	Horse	Sheep	🐐

4. Astrological Enemies

Then there are the astrological enemies of the Horoscope. This is the sign that directly confronts yours in the Astrology Compass. For the Snake, your enemy is the Boar. Note that the enemy does not necessarily harm you; it only means someone of this sign can never be of any real help to you. There is a six year gap between natural enemies.

A marriage between them is not usually recommended. Whatever sincere intentions they have will be short lived and can rarely stand the test of time. Marriage between a Snake and Boar is generally unlikely to bring lasting happiness unless there are other indications in their respective paht chee charts. Pairings between arrows of antagonism are usually discouraged by those who investigate Zodiac compatibilities.

Snakes are advised to refrain from getting involved with a Boar. As a business partnership, the pairing is likely to lead to problems, and in the event of a split, the separation can be acrimonious even if they start out as best friends.

PAIRINGS OF ASTROLOGICAL ENEMIES

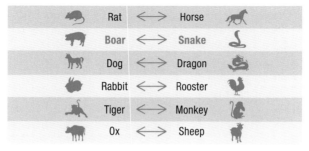

🐀	Rat	⟷	Horse 🐎
🐖	Boar	⟷	Snake 🐍
🐕	Dog	⟷	Dragon 🐉
🐇	Rabbit	⟷	Rooster 🐓
🐅	Tiger	⟷	Monkey 🐒
🐂	Ox	⟷	Sheep 🐐

5. Peach Blossom Links

Each of the Alliance of Allies has a special relationship with one of the four primary signs of Horse, Rat, Rooster and Rabbit in that these are the symbolic representations of love and romance for one Alliance group of animal signs. In the Horoscope, they are referred to as peach blossom animals and the presence of their images in the homes of the matching Alliance of Allies brings Peach Blossom luck which is associated with love and romance.

The Snake belongs to the Alliance of Snake, Rooster and Ox, and they have the Horse as their peach blossom link. The Snake will benefit from associating with anyone born in the Horse year, and will also benefit from placing a **painting or image of a Horse** in the South corner of the house, or in the Snake direction of Southeast.

The **Horse** is the Snake's Peach Blossom Animal,
bringing luck in love and romance.

5. Seasonal Trinity

Another grouping of animal signs creates the four seasonal trinity combinations that bring the luck of seasonal abundance. To many astrology experts, this is regarded as one of the most powerful combinations, and when it exists within a family made up of either parent or both parents) and with one or more children, it indicates that, collectively these family members are strong enough to transform all negative luck indications for the family members that make up the combination for the entire year.

Thus when the annual indications of the year are not favorable, the existence of the seasonal combination of animal signs in any living abode can transform the

SEASONAL TRINITIES OF THE HOROSCOPE

ANIMAL SIGNS	SEASON	ELEMENT	DIRECTION
Dragon, Rabbit, Tiger	Spring	Wood	East
Snake, Horse, Sheep	Summer	Fire	South
Monkey, Rooster, Dog	Autumn	Metal	West
Ox, Rat, Boar	Winter	Water	North

bad luck into better luck especially during the season indicated by the combination.

It is necessary for all 3 animal signs to live together in the same house or to be in the same office working in close proximity for this powerful pattern to work. For greater impact it is better feng shui if they are all using the direction associated with the relevant seasons.

The Snake belongs to the seasonal combination of Summer, a combination which strengthens its links with the Horse, which is the peach blossom animal of the Snake. When a Snake and Horse marry and have a Sheep child for instance, the 3 of them form the trinity of Summer. This means they are not only exceptionally close but also attract the luck of the great summer harvest during the summer season! And because they are a summer grouping, they tend to be very good looking people.

The Snake, Horse and Sheep make up the seasonal combination of Summer.

SNAKE WITH RAT

In 2011, year's energy brings joyful new understanding

Snake continues to hold a special magic for Rat in 2011. This couple will enjoy the benefits of excellent energy vibes brought by auspicious 24 mountain stars. Snake's Life Force and chi strength stay at the same high levels as last year. So the charisma of Snake continues to be mesmerizing. This sign's aura seem to be as awesome this year, as it was in the past year. Who can blame Rat for being unable to resist?

Things are just too good for Rat to succumb to the angry vibrations of the number 3 star. Especially since as a pair they can climb higher than ever. Rat's energy may be weaker than that of Snake, but Rat brings the promise of something huge and awesome for them both. This can be a success of some kind, a new development or a sudden windfall. Nevertheless, it is not an even pairing, and it is Snake who will call the shots whether Rat is aware of it or not. Snake's energy essence is at maximum strength this year. However, the Snake is also a charmer, someone extremely skilful in the art of making his/her partner happy. There is great warmth in this relationship and this has nothing to do with any special affinity of either. Their compatibility arises from their personality types. The Snake sign may be strong and charismatic this year but it does not make Snake arrogant in any way. Indeed Snake is always careful never to make anyone feel inadequate, least of all someone as dear as a loved one. As such, Rat who is generally a lot more egoistic than Snake, often having a tendency towards arrogance, never feels threatened in the company of Snake. This is also the secret of the elegant Snake's great success in most relationships.

The Rat and Snake in their twenties sees the younger 22 year old Snake and the 27 year old Rat enjoying a year filled with auspicious new developments; while a pairing between 39 year old Rat and 34 year old Snake will see them both enjoy a series of big and small successes that turn the year into a happy one. These are the signs who are at the prime of their lives, so they will have the vigor and strength to make quite a lot out of a rather good year for them. For the 51 year old Metal Rat and 46 year old Wood Snake, the outlook appears less glorious. Neither will enjoy very much in terms of new money luck, so things are not as exciting as for the younger pairings. But the relationship stays sound. For this, and other older couples of Rat and Snake, the Rabbit year 2011 is a good time for them to take life a little easier.

SNAKE WITH OX
Allies on a roll
find new reasons for intimacy

These two signs are Zodiac allies and between them is a restful compatibility that scales new levels in 2011. This year, both of you continue to feel at ease with one another and go deeper in your relationship. It promises to be a time when many things ride out smoothly for you and shared aspirations open up new avenues.

> As a couple, this pair is well matched and have plenty to be excited about; and because there is also excellent communication between you, there will be little for you to quarrel or disagree about.

With the Rooster, you form a powerful Alliance of Allies and as a trinity, such as if you have a Rooster child, you will create a simply awesome team. But these 3 animal signs are the intellectuals of the Zodiac. You are quick-witted and intellectually sharp, so there exists between Ox and Snake a very special kind of rapport. Neither of you suffer fools gladly and can sometimes be intellectual snobs. The happy result of this is that you will both be drawn to the same kinds of friends. This adds a special dimension to your relationship. The drawback however is the uneven levels of energy. In 2011 Snake continues to be very high energy while Ox finds it hard to keep up. This arises from Snake's high Life Force and Spirit Essence. As such, although Ox enjoys *Big Auspicious* success luck, Snake not only has no trouble keeping up, it will more than likely outshine Ox. Physically and mentally, Snake will perform better; and socially, Snake will also be more in demand.

Ox has to work at shaking off some jealousy creeping in. It is unfortunate but Snake's star seems to be shining very bright indeed and Ox must depend on its strong backbone to make sure it does not wilt in the glare of Snake's mesmerizing personality. Ox is not by nature a jealous person. Being supremely confident with a powerful sense of self worth, it is likely that given its own excellent indications this year, Ox will simply bask in the reflected glory of Snake's star power.

It is only when work and business are going badly that feelings of inadequacy arise thus affecting the relationship. Fortunately, this is quite unlikely to happen in 2011. If this pair are married, they would be too busy to suffer the fall-out from jealousies arising. Besides, unlike last year when the *Star of External Romance* was casting its influence, this year there is nothing of this sort disturbing either Ox or Snake.

SNAKE WITH TIGER
Strength in good teamwork

In 2011, Snake once again charms Tiger, who is mesmerized by the easy confidence and stylish posture of this Fire sign. It is understandable, as Snake is enjoying another great year, and its aura is so strong that it evokes admiration from Tiger, when before there might have been envy and even latent resentment. This year antipathy changes to awe, and for some, it can even become a fixation.

The Snake has a strong aura in 2011, exuding a self-assured personality that many find enticing, and the Tiger simply cannot resist. It is just as well that in 2011, the Snake who is single and available is open to propositions, and thus will not be averse to any overtures made by Tiger. In fact, it is possible that Tiger's own self assurance will make Snake sit up and take notice.

A pairing of these two signs manifests heaven's magic and it will be a wonderful time for them in 2011. As a couple, they will cause some fabulous benefits to emerge. There is good teamwork between them, excellent mindfulness to their commitment to each other and an admirable cooperation - all of which suggest they can work together.

Tiger is able to identify with Snake's enthusiasm for life, and both experience an exhilaration that reflects Snake's inner energy. Snake puts many signs to shame this year (without doing anything other than be itself) and it is easy for just about anyone to feel comparatively inadequate, if one allows comparisons to cloud a relationship with this sign.

> The Tiger thankfully is feeling strong and so is able to relate to Snake at a transformative level. It is like heaven working its magic on the Tiger and Snake pair, bringing joyousness to a challenging and stimulating relationship. The Snake happily responds to Tiger's overtures.

Those of you already married to each other will find that 2011 brings a renewal of past attraction that manifests a new phase in your relationship. Last year was not good, but this year, Tiger and Snake rekindle a trust that had gone missing for some time.

The improved sentiments come from both signs being affected by the good influence of heaven energy; plus this year, their feng shui chart numbers are extremely compatible and auspicious as well. This augurs well for them both.

SNAKE WITH RABBIT
A cool relationship that goes nowhere

In 2011, this relationship is plagued by the coolness of the Snake, and any coming together is likely to dissolve in the chilly atmosphere generated by the Snake's distance. This couple had some happier times last year, but in 2011, Snake cools off and starts to distance itself.

> Much of the lack of compatibility comes from their extremely disparate energies in 2011. Snake is strong, vibrant, confident and in search of adventure and new worlds to conquer. Rabbit is just the opposite, suffering from apathy and coping with some trials and tribulations that force it to focus on maintenance rather than growth. There is just no meeting of minds here, not unless Rabbit is prepared for heartbreak and disappointment. This is a relationship that benefits neither of you, at least not this year.

The Rabbit and Snake have never been very compatible. It is quite difficult expecting them to ignite any great passion together, and in 2011, it is unlikely that Snake would respond in a positive way to Rabbit. Snake may be riding high but it is reserving tis charm for someone equally ambitious.

Rabbit is still going through a low energy year while Snake is high voltage, a star in every sense. This makes such a difference to their respective years. There is simply no meeting of minds here, unless Rabbit finds Snake an exciting challenge and exerts all its charm to woo the Snake. If this is the situation, then Rabbit, take note that the Snake finds sexy people irresistible! Snake also respond to flattery and seduction, and to confident people; it is thus important to come across a winner and to be intellectually stimulating if you want to snare the heart of a Snake.

But Rabbit should appreciate that in a romantic entanglement with Snake, should they become a couple, it is a relationship that will always have its ups and downs, and maybe more downs. Rabbit must accept that Snake can freeze out of the relationship with little warning. Sad but true!

Rabbit simply cannot take things easy in the company of Snake. This can easily deteriorate into annoyance, with Rabbit becoming disillusioned. So on balance, it is advisable not to let this relationship go too far. If you are already married, try to find common ground so that shared interests become the unifying force that cements your relationship together.

SNAKE WITH DRAGON
Beneficial to forge an alliance

The Dragon forges a very special relationship with the Snake, who in 2011 continues to be riding incredibly high on a wave of fresh new creativity. Snake is Dragon's special ally and together, these two signs make magic of their lives. They are at their best when working together towards a common goal; their energies are very much in sync and their thought processes in tune and beating to the same rhythm.

> With Snake, Dragon is always practical and grounded, having ambitions but also able to see the practical side of situations and outcomes. These two signs are thus very compatible and suited for each other. It is however an alliance of equals, with neither having the upper hand or being in a dominating posture, although in 2011, the energy of the Snake far outpaces that of the Dragon.

The Dragon is mesmerized by the magical aura of the Snake personality so there is not just love and romance but also respect. The Snake brings out all that is best in the feisty Dragon and there are many triumphant moments and shared joys that both can relate to. Even without having too much in common, this is a couple that can adapt to one another's passions and friends. Snake's luck in 2011 continues to be at a high level, and Snake brings benefits to those who are around its sphere of influence. A Dragon married to a Snake spouse is sure to take strength from the Snake, so this is a good pairing. In 2011, the Dragon is weak in terms of its inner chi, but not to worry, as Snake has enough inner power for both.

This arises from the special nature of their relationship; the Snake and Dragon together create the *House of Magic and Spirituality*. The energised empowered Snake takes the lead in 2011, while the loud and boisterous Dragon is more than happy to play second fiddle.

The married Dragon/Snake will see their marriage move to new levels as they build on what they already have. This is a year that favors those of you in business together or who may be working on the same project. Your energies with each other are always complementary, so good ideas issue forth. The couples made up of Dragons/Snakes in their thirties and fifties do best in 2011, while the other pairings depend more on Snake taking the lead, while Dragon should just roll along and enjoy the ride.

SNAKE WITH SNAKE
Sexual highs in a terrific 2011

Snake's optimism and high energy is infectious, and it finds resonance with its own sign; there is an easy sense of compatibility when two Snakes come together this year, enjoying the promise of both big and small manifestations of good fortune. There is also a great deal of amiability, and give and take - all fostered by the pathway being smooth through the year. The only time one might find the other a trite tiresome will be in the month April 2011 and perhaps also in January 2012. You could also be rather quarrelsome in June when the fires of summer cause you both to get rather hot under the collar. It is a good month to take a deep breath and maybe not see too much of each other.

By and large, this will be a relatively happy pairing and it seems the year is almost conspiring to bring you many moments of great bliss and ecstasy. There is success luck and pleasant surprises that bring good news unexpectedly. There will thus be renewed passion between Snakes who might have become a little tired of one another.

In most years, when Snake's energy is lethargic or weak, Snakes tend to be very indifferent towards its own sign. Usually, their togetherness as a couple arises more from a sense of good companionship than by any feelings of passion between them. Snakes are generally drawn towards the excitement of adventure so they would look on another Snake as being too understated.

But move beyond the obvious and Snake could well find its counterpart has a lot more to offer. In 2011 there is a likelihood that a Snake pairing up with another Snake will discover new worlds and new interests. They will delve deeper into one another's psyche, and in so doing, forge a new understanding.

Snakes married to each other will love the energy of the new year and will happily seek out each other's company where before they might have been quite content living separate lives, each with his/her own program. But all this goodwill and newfound passion is not to suggest that Snake will not respond should there be temptations. In 2011, Snake is attractive and alluring, so there is always the danger of outside interests getting the better of them.

Those married to another Snake would do well to be alert to temptations either for themselves or their partner, and nip any danger of infidelity in the bud! Snakes are notoriously unfaithful, but they are also great at simply slithering away when things get complicated.

SNAKE WITH HORSE
A Relationship
that transforms Small into Big

For the Snake, the Horse is all good news! True, the energy of this magnificent creature cannot compare in either radiance or shine to the great lustre of the Snake in 2011; nevertheless, the Horse has its own store of high octane energy which attracts even better and bigger luck to its side. In fact, in 2011, Horse will tend to over exert and eventually feel the heaviness of reducing energy. But Horse benefits Snake's already good fortune indications. So this is a pair that is great for one another in 2011.

For this reason, Horse is as attracted to Snake as vice versa. This is a year when being with a Horse transforms Snake's good fortune luck from small into big. This means that small gains become big gains and small profits and successes become big ones. It is all very beneficial indeed.

For Horse, Snake's store of chi energy will pump new adrenalin into its system. It is indeed a very perfect match. These are two Fire signs that do best together during the summer months. In 2011, their best month will indeed be in June, when star numbers combine beautifully and feng shui winds are also in sync.

Those of you Snakes married to a Horse will surely have something great to look forward to in the middle of the new year.

For those of you who are still single and meeting for the first time, the attraction between you two will be quite instantaneous. The 33 year old Earth Horse cannot resist the 34 year old Fire Snake, and both really are at the height of their energy levels. It is only important to pace yourselves. Having too much of a good thing, especially when there is so much Fire between you two, can be exhausting. You run the risk of a burn out... so do take good care not to overexert yourselves. The couple in their forties will be the most well suited, while the younger Horse and Snake in their twenties would simply tire of each other.

The Horse must remember that the Snake's aura is formidable and its chi levels very high in 2011. Since the Horse is its peach blossom animal, the Snake is likely to tire the Horse out by quite a margin; these two signs light fires for one another, so things can well get too hot for both. Nevertheless, this is an endearing relationship; passion here is real and affection is genuine; and with the winds favoring you as a pair, the year should end as good as it begins.

SNAKE WITH SHEEP
Suppressed animosity between these two

The 2011 distribution of chi energy around the Zodiac cycle repeats the scenario of last year for this pair; Snake's vitality is at its zenith while Sheep's energy is at a low ebb. One is all fired up and eager to savor life, while the other is distracted, limiting its attention and energy almost exclusively to its own inner world. This is a mismatched pair having their own hidden agendas, and whatever animosity simmering beneath could well get unstuck and rise up into the open. Not a good thing to happen!

It is hard for these two different signs to find common ground in 2011 mainly because of the way the winds are blowing; there are different aspirations and standards pulling them apart. While Snake is feeling adventurous and optimistic, Sheep is coming to terms with its own feelings of inadequacy. Sheep is easily exhausted most of the time, while Snake is flexing its muscles eager to try new things.

Energy, rhythm and even the pace of their thinking are at odds. So if you are getting together for the first time, better to find comfort and love elsewhere. Snake may be feeling passionate, but the simpering emotional type is not what Snake wants. Sheep is feeling sentimental and romantic quite unlike the Snake, so their view of love and romance are quite different. There is little to pull these two together. Even if they did have something in common on which to build a potentially satisfying relationship, it is unlikely to last. Both signs get turned off when bored, and both get bored easily. Snake tends to be intellectually snobbish while Sheep tends to be materialistic. They respect different skills and strengths, and if they live together, it is sure to permeate and spoil their relationship

The older of the two signs probably has the patience to live through their relationship if they happen to be married. The 68 year old Water Sheep for instance, though suffering from failing health, will be tolerant and indulgent of its Snake partner. But the Metal Sheep cannot be bothered. From the viewpoint of Snake, those in their forties, fifties and sixties who are married, (the Wood, Water and Fire Snake respectively) will simply not hesitate to fool around and cultivate outside love interests. Suspicion, frustrations and repressed anger cause aggravations of this couple. But Sheep is just as likely to succumb to outside temptations. So unless there is an understanding between them, it seems better to create their own private worlds away from each other.

SNAKE WITH MONKEY
Lending strength to a secret friend

These are secret friends that possess a very deep and lingering affection for one another, and the longer you are together, the stronger will be the bonds that bind you. As a pair, you can draw strength from each other and achieve some pretty amazing things. In 2011, the strength is rather one-sided however, with most of the giving coming from Snake. But you are happy to be the nurturing one in this relationship.

You will find that you genuinely enjoy one another's company, as a result of which you are inseparable. Snake and Monkey cannot endure a long distance relationship and this is where 2011 can offer some challenges. Snake will find that it is a year when travel brings great work-related benefits, as a result of which there is plenty of potential for short but regular separations between this pair. This tears at the relationship and can cause stress and strain to the Monkey. Here, it is all up to Snake who calls the shots. In 2011, Snake is going through a much better year than Monkey, so it is Snake who needs to be sensitive and who will need to weigh options and decide accordingly. Snake needs to understand that Monkey is feeling a lot more amorous this year, more so than ever before.

It is true to say that for many born in the year of the Monkey, they are going through their "nesting period" so domestic issues are high in their priorities. Snake on the other hand is just beginning to rediscover the joys of being more active socially.

Snake is also going through a time of great popularity and a blossoming of opportunities provide temptation to party, travel and basically be more sociable. Ordinarily, Monkey will be up to it, but this year, Monkey prefers the quiet solitude of one-on-one romance. There is a need here for great sensitivity between them and understanding as well.

The 67 year old Wood Monkey goes through a time of indecision and will depend on its partner the 70 year old Metal Snake, seeing Snake here as a tower of strength to lean on. The pair in their fifties, the 59 year old Water Snake and 55 year old Fire Monkey will enjoy fruitful year when there will be more pluses than negatives. In the case of the 43 year old Earth Monkey, it will be the 46 year old Wood Snake who pulls them through some challenging situations. Meanwhile, the pair in their thirties will find the year harder going, while the younger couple will simply have a ball, enjoying good times.

SNAKE WITH ROOSTER
Helping an ally overcome afflictions

In 2011, the empowered Snake extends a strong and hefty helping hand to the embattled and afflicted Rooster! This is because the Year of the Rabbit brings wonderfully vigorous yang energy to Snake, but brings some negative feng shui winds to Rooster. It is just as well that the inner essence and Life Force of Rooster is at a high level, making it strong enough to cope with the *Three Killings* and the confrontation with the *Tai Sui,* but having the borrowed luck from Snake will make a crucial difference.

> The energy patterns of these two allies bring some challenges into this relationship. This is because while Snake's horoscope luck is truly quite formidable, neither the feng shui winds blowing nor the cosmic constellation of the 24 mountains are helping Rooster. As a result, there is a great disparity in the respective energies of this pair.

Snake's Southeast location is blessed by the heavenly star of 6, while Rooster's West location is afflicted by the *Natural Disaster Star* brought by the 24 mountains. However, the feng shui chart brings the star of 9 to the Rooster, so 2011 is a year when despite obstacles and bad winds, Rooster will emerge stronger than ever, especially the Rooster that has the help of the Snake. Having said that, the year is not necessarily pleasant. There will be stress and strains, tensions and even misunderstandings in the relationship. But you need to hang in there and stay committed to each other.

This year's events will test Snake, who is bound to feel that Rooster's baggage is a little heavy. Resentment of some kind might indeed set in, but Snake must not make the mistake of writing a troubled Rooster off. Like the phoenix, the Rooster will surprise everyone by its staying power and also by the number of things it can literally pull out of its hat to transform negative situations into positive ones.

It is a good thing that between this pair is a big supply of mutual respect, devotion and love. So they will interact at a level that transcends even the spiritual. There is good psychic awareness between them, so that all through 2011, the Snake and Rooster will trust and lift one another to new heights of understanding and steadfastness.

SNAKE WITH DOG
Attraction is mutual and full of sparks

In the year 2011, Snake has plenty of fun with Dog. Their personalities are in sync as both glow in the limelight fuelled by a continuous momentum of good times and even better vibrations.

> This is not a pair that naturally gets drawn to each other, but in 2011, their strong auras glow with a brightness that acts like a natural antenna for one another. So attraction between them is mutual, generating lots of sparks and electricity.

In 2011 both the Snake and Dog possess some powerful energy brought by the feng shui winds of the year. As a couple, you can keep up with each other, and you will find pleasure in doing the same things. It is not at all like the previous year, so if you are meeting one another for the first time, it is sure to be a blast!

Traditionally, the Snake and Dog do not have much that draws them together. You are not astrologically linked in any way and there is little to bond the Snake to the Dog personality. So the relationship will find its own comfort zone at a relatively shallow level. But this should not in any way put you off each other, and happily does not do so in 2011. Both of you are perfectly acceptable of the fact that it is not necessary to operate at such deep levels. For both of you, the year 2011 can be as superficial as anything, but you will still enjoy all the goodies that come to you both. And if finding one another is the highlight of your year, you are practical enough to simply sit back and enjoy.

In 2011, Dog is strengthened by the power of 8. Success luck is at an all-time high and relationship luck is also strong. Snake resonates with Dog's optimistic attitude this year and finds the Dog personality very attractive.

If Snake and Dog are married, both experience a renewed sense of discovery. Snake responds to the promise of new excitement offered by an empowered Dog, so there is a chance for the year to be a lot more pleasant than last year.

The good thing about these two signs is their practical and down-to-earth attitude towards life and relationships in that whatever bad vibes may have been created in the past, they can shrug them off and look ahead instead. This is the key to their happiness through the year.

SNAKE WITH BOAR
Too High Octane for Laid-Back Boar

The Snake and Boar are old adversaries, being natural enemies of the Zodiac, so that even when there is initial attraction between this pair, it generally does not last and cannot stand the influence of the astrological forces that pull them towards other people whose signs have greater resonance with them. The Snake and Boar are just not made for each other.

In any case, 2011 is a great and powerful year for the Snake, and this is not a turn-on for the Boar person, who is sure to be intimidated. But the Boar is also enjoying a good year and feeling strong, as a result of which this pair meeting for the first time could well end up pressing all the right buttons for one another.

If so however, do not think that it will be long lasting. But you are both enjoying a very positive time and there is no harm at all in indulging one another. Just do not expect it to lead to any kind of genuine commitment from either party to the other. It will not take long for the Boar to discover that Snake is simply too intellectual, too high octane and maybe even too demanding for its peace of mind.

In 2010, Snake is strong and Boar is no less so. The Boar benefits from the power of 8 in the feng shui chart and it is this that resonates with the Snake's power of 6, both being white numbers. This is the source of their attraction for one another in 2011.

But the Snake should be aware that while the Boar personality is basically quite accommodating and easy going, its element is Water which can douse your Fire! The thing to note is that Boar's element of Water is a source of great strength for the Boar and it is Water that helps the Boar take fullest advantage of all the good indications brought by the winds of the feng shui chart.

> Between this pair, communication is limited and the Boar has the knack of aggravating the Snake, always talking at a tangent. Should this pair be in a marriage, it is a sad mismatch, although in 2011, the energy of the year will bring them to a new high in their relationship.

This is a year when everything is going right for both the Snake and Boar; both will be brimming with confidence and vitality, so it is advisable to simply sit back and enjoy the year.

Snake's Monthly
Horoscope 2011

Part 5

Snake Goes Through
A Magical High Energy Year

This year is an excellent one for the Snake, characterized by heavenly luck and opportunities dropping out of the sky. The Metal energy that flies into your sector is well under your control, and with amazing Life Force and chi essence indications, this allows you to convert many good opportunities into real and tangible success.

Prosperity, power and good relationships are all up for grabs if you're hungry enough; but it is also a year when you will need the help of others. Your personal luck is extremely enviable, but if you try to do everything alone, you will find truly big success hard to come by. Surround yourself with friends and allies, and make the most of help offered to you by those in positions to provide it.

1ST MONTH
February 4th - March 5th 2011

NATURAL AVERSION FOR FRAUDSTERS

The auspicious Metal energy of the heavenly star is joined by the violent star in your sector this month, creating an excess of Metal energy, leading to real danger of losing money and being cheated. Avoid investing heavily this month and focus on keeping yourself and your money safe. There is also some danger of physical injury, so put some focus on personal safety for the next four weeks. Avoid overspending or being wasteful this month; some of you could feel the pinch when some un-expected expenses crop up. Your luck this year is however quite remarkable, giving you astute and accurate instincts. If you feel uneasy over any-thing, back away. Don't let conventional common sense override your gut-feel, which will get you out of more than one sticky situation this month.

WORK & CAREER - A Trying Time

The following few weeks may be trying for the Snake at work. You could find yourself losing your cool and getting into arguments and mental tussles with co-workers. Control your temper. The calmer you keep, the better things tend to work out for you. Beware of challengers and backstabbers in the office. Even friends can turn on you when the situation suits them. This is a precarious month when you'll need to play your cards right. Striking the right balance when it comes to relationships at work will prove disproportionately important this month. Make sure you have a **Rooster** on your workdesk to shield against falling victim to petty office politics. And don't give anyone the chance to criticize you by making sure you don't put too many wrong feet forward.

BUSINESS – *Pre-empt Mistakes*

Keep this month as quiet as possible. It is better to leave major decision-making till next month when your luck improves. You may find your senses dulled this month, and you may miss things that would otherwise be so obvious. Not a good time to make too many strategic decisions, particularly ones that can

Display a **Rooster** on your workdesk this month to protect against office politics and intrigues.

have far-reaching consequences. Pre-empt mistakes by thinking everything through carefully. On-the-fly decisions are probably not a good idea this month. Avoid entering into new partnerships particularly with entities you don't know so well. It is easy to get cheated as you are afflicted by the robbery star this month. Display the **Rhino and Elephant** with **blue water globe** in the Southeast to minimize losses.

LOVE & RELATIONSHIPS - *Prickly*
You're short on luck when it comes to your love life, so best not to try anything fanciful or you could fall flat on your face. This is not the best of times to woo your sweetheart or wear your heart on your sleeve. If you're in the midst of pursuing someone, concentrate on saying and doing the right things. It is easy to be perceived to be thoughtless, even when you have the best of intentions. Beware also of quarrelsome energies lurking in the sidelines. A simple lover's tiff can do more damage than you realize. If you find yourself sparring with your partner, keep it lighthearted and don't hit below the belt. Watch your words this month.

EDUCATION - *Don't be Overly Sensitive*
You may find yourself in some tricky situations when it comes to relationships with friends at school. Don't be overly sensitive and give others the benefit of the doubt.

2ND MONTH
March 6th - April 4th 2011

HOOKING UP WITH PEOPLE OF INFLUENCE

You have a much better month to look forward to this month. The obstacles and difficulties of last month evaporate into thin air and you can start to relax again. Aggravations disappear and relationships with others improve. This month the Snake person benefits incredibly from hooking up with the right people. Nurture new relationships and make the effort to get closer to others you may want to do things with in the future. You could well find yourself involved in a mutually very beneficial partnership with an unexpected entity this month. Let the ambitious nature within you come forward and apply yourself fully to all areas of your life. The next four weeks hold out much promise, so don't rest on your laurels. Use the month wisely.

WORK & CAREER - *Don't Be Overly Humble*

Teamwork is vitally important this month. Working well with your colleagues will ensure you get the work done well, fast and without envious or bitter rivals sabotaging your efforts. Make an extra effort to be super nice to everyone; you need them on your side. You could catch the eye of the boss this month, but don't invoke feelings of jealousy among your peers or things won't ride out as smoothly as they could otherwise. Keep your mind on the job and look out for situations where you can use your skill set to the best of your ability. Don't be overly self-deprecating. This is a time when being overly humble won't do you any favors. Step up to your responsibilities and take on a few more. There is a lot of promise when it comes to your career this month, so seize the initiative and make the most of it.

BUSINESS – *Many Opportunities*

There are many opportunities in business this month. The stars in your chart are lined up to bring you as much help as you need. You are able to achieve a lot this month if you set your mind to it. Make good use of your generals and don't try to do everything alone. You benefit from the luck of good teamwork so put that to good use. Don't just delegate orders, make the most of the talents within your company. There may be a superstar or two in your team; recognizing them now could awaken something incredibly exciting. Give credit where it's due and everyone will benefit. Partnerships struck up this month are likely to do well, so if there is a good fit, go for it. But don't do anyone any favors. It must be a mutually beneficial relationship or things will just fizzle out.

LOVE & RELATIONSHIPS - *Love Burgeons*

Things look good when it comes to love and matters of the heart. Those of you single and looking could find someone to set your sights on this month. Don't resist if there is chemistry. Being too cautious about taking the plunge into a relationship could see you miss out on something truly quite special. Love burgeons from the most unlikely of places this month. You may have admirers you've never even noticed in the past. Open your eyes and you could discover that the person you've been looking for has always been right there. For those of you who are married, you can look forward to a romantic month ahead when reconnecting with your partner brings much joy.

EDUCATION - *A Prolific Time*

A prolific time for the student Snake! Use this time to learn and absorb as much as possible. Clarity of thought gives rise to the kind of understanding that could have proved elusive for some time. You benefit from the advice and counsel of older and wiser people this month. Make it a point to get close to your teachers and professors, and you will gain much more than just what's on the syllabus.

3RD MONTH
April 5th - May 5th 2011

AVOIDING THE FIVE YELLOW

The five yellow flies into your home sector this month, marring the good luck the year in general brings. This month it is better to lie low and stay quiet. Avoid gambling or risk-taking. There could be some small misfortunes on the cards but you will

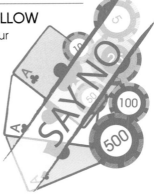

cope well as long as you are well prepared. Don't let small setbacks in your life become issues. Turning molehills into mountains will have you falling into the trap of the malicious five yellow. Your Life Force and Spirit Essence are first rate this year, so this should be enough to ensure you don't suffer more than a few road bumps along the way. There could be some seemingly exciting opportunities beckoning, but it is better to wait until next month before acting on anything. Ventures started this month have little chance of success in the long run, so be a little patient and hold your horses.

WORK & CAREER - *Small Setbacks*

There may be some disappointment on the cards when it comes to your career. Something you've been expecting to turn out a certain way could turn out differently. Don't let small setbacks get you down. Instead, use every experience as a learning process. Keep your desires in check and delay any grand plans you may have been hatching. This is a time to maintain a low profile and to keep your talents to yourself. There could be some politicking and backbiting at the office, and plenty of it aimed at you. But responding could merely make things worse. Wear a **jade cicada** and wear a **Five Element Pagoda** in gold. This will minimize the damage the Five Yellow can cause. Because it is difficult for you to win this month, don't raise a challenge. Instead, bide your time and look forward to a better time next month.

BUSINESS - *Don't Overreact*

Avoid going into business with friends this month; you're likely to lose money or damage a perfectly good friendship. This is a time when as much as possible you should keep business ticking over as usual. Not a good time for expansion, diversification or trying new things. If there is any problem, try not to overreact. Dramatizing an issue will only make a problem look worse than it is, and could cause other problems to sprout up elsewhere. Use this time to consolidate your position, and save your efforts for next month.

LOVE & RELATIONSHIPS – *Stay Lighthearted*
Avoid discussing heavy topics with your partner this month or you're bound to end up bickering. Even if you don't agree with everything your partner expounds, always try to compromise. Quell your dogmatic nature; being overly stubborn will just make the both of you miserable. If you keep things lighthearted when it comes to romantic relationships, you're likely to have a much more enjoyable time this month. Be flexible and accommodating and you'll not only find your love relationships go better, friendships also thrive this way. For the Snake on the lookout, this is not the most promising of times to snare a mate. And if you're not looking for something serious, you'll probably come across a lot more attractive to your potential mate.

EDUCATION – *Lone Work Turns Our Better*
You do better studying alone than in groups this month. Don't become too dependent on anyone else when completing your assignments. If you focus, things will come to you. You might become quite a loner when it comes to your school work this month, but this is not necessarily a bad thing, and in fact could be just what you needed all this time.

4TH MONTH
May 6th - June 5th 2011

LOVE IS IN THE AIR; ROMANCE FLOURISHES!

This is a fabulous month for love! Your star combinations this month causes romance to blossom for you, and new relationships struck up now have a good chance of becoming the real thing. A fabulous time for lovers to tie the knot, for getting engaged or for taking a relationship to the next level. Those of you already happily married will find their spouse a great asset this month. A strong partnership is the key to moving forward, and the next four weeks holds out the potential and promise of your spouse and yourself creating unbreakable new bonds. There is plenty of happiness indicated in your chart right now, so there is much to look forward to.

WORK & CAREER – *Indispensable*

You're in high spirits this month and this rubs off on everyone you come into contact with. You work well with others and your contribution as a team member becomes quite indispensable. Whether your input comes in the form of a genuinely good new idea, an astute observation, a good judgment call or simply much-needed humor, you're welcome in any circle right now. You rub everyone up the right way, making you as popular with your colleagues and subordinates as with your boss and superiors. You could find yourself in the running for a managerial position or meaningful promotion. You're everyone's best friend, but while you should remain approachable and warm, refrain from becoming too close to anybody or engaging in gossip or this could be your undoing this month. Beware also of office romances, which could be tempting for those of you who work late, long hours.

BUSINESS - *Relationships Rule*

Nurture the relationships you make this month; they promise to form an important network of contacts for things you will be doing in the near future. Business luck for you hinges on your personality and how you get along with others this month. This is a time when your natural charm and appeal can get anyone on your side.

Your instincts are good right now so you can trust them when making decisions. Don't ignore a gut feel and don't let common sense override your initial reaction when it comes to business deals and decisions. When something feels right, go with the flow and go in with confidence. When something feels wrong, walk away no matter how attractive it is made to sound.

LOVE & RELATIONSHIPS – *Full of Passion*

A sublime month when it comes to passion and romance. Single Snakes have a ball of a time this month and are likely to be whisked off their feet by some charming admirer. Relationships get struck up easily but you may want to consider carefully before committing or you could miss out on something better that comes along. But whether it's something serious or short-lived you're looking for, there will be many memorable moments for you this month. The married Snake however has to be a little bit careful. There is danger of external romance and while some charismatic outsider could turn on the charm, don't let yourself fall into the trap of infidelity. It could lead to huge problems later on so resist temptation if it presents itself.

EDUCATION – *Newfound Enthusiasm*

You feel in control of your circumstances and become particularly enthusiastic about your work and assignments. For the young Snake, your studies suddenly become more important to you, and this shows up in moments of brilliance in the classroom. Those of you sitting exams have the potential to do very well indeed. Activate this luck with a **Good Education** amulet.

5TH MONTH
June 6th - July 6th 2011

AVOIDING CONFLICTS BY SLITHERING AWAY

The quarrelsome star rules the energies this month, bringing you into regular conflict with your friends and loved ones. Try to hold your temper and keep your cool, or you're the one who will lose out the most. When you feel something caustic at the edge of your tongue, hold back. Silent wars are definitely better than verbal ones this month. Don't say anything that can't be unsaid. The people around you may seem to you to be overly sensitive, but instead of shoving the blame, take a look at yourself. If you can try to be more amiable yourself, you'll find everyone else following suit. Some quality alone time will do you a world of good this month.

WORK & CAREER - *Keep Your Cool*

You're likely to face some obstacles to career advancement this month, so keep your ambitions to yourself. You may find it difficult to deal with others, particularly those of the same gender as you. Some developments at work may really make your blood boil, but if you can keep your cool, you can come out ahead. This is a dangerous month to make known your ill feelings towards others. If you have to bitch, do it to your dog, not to someone who can repeat what you say. This will only get you into hotter soup. The best strategy this month is not to take on too much, and to avoid working too closely with others. Be a team player but avoid poking your nose into other people's business. Things improve next month when you won't find everything riling you so easily.

BUSINESS – *Listen to the Opinions of Others*

Obstacles sprout up out of nowhere, putting the brakes on the plans laid long ago. Be adaptable to the situation. The more stubborn you are in wanting to stick to the plan, the worse things will turn out. Listen to the opinions of others. You may not be in the mood to be disagreed with, but this month, others really could have some better ideas than you. The smartest thing for you to do is to give these outside proposals a chance. There's a fair probability you may have missed something that someone else can pick up on. If you work at being a better team player – even if you are the boss – you'll find things turning out better than you expect. Those of you who remain obstinate however could be digging a deeper hole for yourselves.

LOVE & RELATIONSHIPS - *Squabbles*

Petty squabbles are the order of the day this month and especially in close relationships, you're likely to let loose. The more intimate you are with your partner, the more chance of an explosion of some sort. Work out your differences and don't go to bed angry. Allowing arguments to fester inside you will only make things worse. Carry the **Ping peace amulet** or the **Fire Gold Magic talisman** this month to conquer the irksome energies of the number 3 star. Because this Wood star flies into the Southeast, it gets strengthened even more, making it more dangerous.

Don't allow yourself to empower it by falling for the bait. This month it is vitally important to be even more understanding than usual.

EDUCATION - *A Trying Time*

This is a trying time for the young Snake. There are more assignments than ever and deadlines to meet, cranking up your stress levels. This could lead to some tension with friends who expect more of your time than you can give. Don't be talked into abandoning your work for your social life, or you'll get yourself even more stressed out when your backlog builds up.

Carry the **Fire Gold talisman** this month to counter the quarrelsome energies that plague your chart.

6TH MONTH
July 7th - Aug 7th 2011

MIGHT SUCCUMB TO AIR-BORNE VIRUSES

Watch your health this month as the illness star has flown into your sector, making you more vulnerable to falling sick. You're susceptible to the common cold, flu and other viruses making the rounds. Boost your immunity with vitamins and by eating well. Don't be tempted to start on some fad diet; it won't do you any good and could lower your immune system and make you quite ill! If you're looking to lose some weight, sign up for a proper program or do it through regular exercise. For the workhorses among you, don't overdo things. If you're feeling under the weather, take a break. Pushing ahead regardless of how you're feeling won't make you any more productive, and if you have to take time off work to recover, then you'll really lose out.

WORK & CAREER - *Plan Well*

No big changes this month when it comes to work, except you may be feeling a little less industrious than usual. It is easy to become sluggish if you allow yourself to start. Make it to work late one day and you could find yourself doing it more and more. Don't let it get to a stage when people start to take notice. If you need to catch up on sleep, have early nights or do it at weekends. Don't try to make up lost slumber in the mornings. Waking up late will only render your mornings unproductive, spiraling downwards into tighter and tighter deadlines and debilitating stress. If there's a lot to get done, plan properly before you get started. Spend a little time figuring out the best way to do something rather than jumping straight in every time. This way you'll expend less energy, be more efficient, and less careless.

BUSINESS - *Keep Your Focus*

Use this month to build on your current strengths rather than trying to develop new ones. Don't spread yourself too thin or involve yourself in too much that you can't give your focused attention to any one thing. This month, being a specialist probably pays off more than having a foot in everything. When making decisions, don't be tentative. If you cannot decide with decisiveness, it is better to wait till next month before making a decision. There are some good relationships waiting to be built and developed this month. Make the effort to socialize and to keep in touch with good contacts made. Some new business associates could also become great friends this month. There may be some good opportunities of strategic tie-ups; if these present themselves, consider them carefully. There is good money to be made this way. You enjoy the power of partnerships this month.

LOVE & RELATIONSHIPS – *Romantic*

Snakes who are married or in steady relationships benefit from their partners this month. You get good moral support from them, and for some of you, also financial support. The Snake personality is good at dominating a relationship without appearing to do so; you put this to good effect this month, but do so with a genuine heart, so partner doesn't even realize you're taking charge, and if they do, they don't mind. Gone are the quarrelsome vibes of last month and you can play happy families again. For those of you who've been married some years, this is a good time to rekindle the flames of passion. Be romantic again and it could lead you to some truly magical places this month.

EDUCATION – *Avoid Dangerous Sports*

Get enough sleep. The worst thing you can do to yourself is to starve yourself from enough rest. Your life may be very full at the moment but it is important to recharge, especially when you have the illness star in your chart.

7TH MONTH
Aug 8th - Sept 7th 2011

ROMPING AHEAD AND WINNING

Victory luck is on your side this month, allowing you to get ahead of the competition in almost any circumstances. This is an exciting month indeed! Grasp with both hands new opportunities that come your way; don't be too slow to react or they could slip away. As well as the victory star, this month you also enjoy a most auspicious Ho Tu combination in your chart. This bodes very well for the month. Start off on the right note and the next four weeks will roll out according to plan. Don't allow yourself to get angry, jealous or petty this month. Be super nice, bend over backwards to help others, and it will all come back to you very soon.

WORK & CAREER - *New Niches*

Even if you're teetering on the brink of boredom with your job, this month will see you finding new opportunities and new niches, transforming your career into something fresh and exciting with tons of potential. If you've been considering a change of career for a while, this month could be the time you decide once and for all whether or not to take the plunge. If you don't see a clear cut future, or the path ahead no longer excites you in your current job, some of you may well be thinking about looking elsewhere. Some of you have that decision made for you, if you are headhunted with an offer that's hard to refuse. Your chart indicates superlative luck this month, so whatever you ultimately decide, chances are it will turn out good.

BUSINESS – *Avenues for Growth*

There are many avenues for growth, and this is the time to decide on a few to pursue. This is a month when new initiatives will not only suggest themselves, but will enthuse and motivate you in your work. Getting more hands-on with the business will stimulate your mind and bring new purpose to your life. Don't be afraid to take a few risks. There is plenty of good fortune on your side to ensure you don't get yourself burnt in the process. Having said that, don't put all your eggs in one basket. Diversifying risk is always a good idea.

Operationally speaking, it is a good idea to allow ideas from others to make it to the drawing board. While you may want to exert your moral authority as boss, don't wield absolute power. Let others shine as well. This will make you a better leader, and gain you greater respect from those who work for and with you.

LOVE & RELATIONSHIPS – *Young at Heart*

You learn to appreciate your partner in new ways this month, a month which is all about shedding the old and looking forward to the new. Be young again. Try new things! Take suggestions from your partner, maybe even take up a new hobby together. When you do more than just share a bed, the two of you will find yourselves really connecting like soul mates. This is an excellent month for Snake people to get married, get engaged or start a family.

EDUCATION – *Fabulous*

You have fabulous education luck this month. Seize the initiative to engage in every learning opportunity you can. Your stars this month are particularly conducive for learning and improving oneself. Enhance luck in this area of your life by displaying **five glitter lamps** in the five element colours in the Southeast of your living room or study room, and keep these lamps turned on for at least three hours each day. This will help crystallize things for you and may even gain you a scholarship if you are applying for one.

8TH MONTH
Sept 8th - Oct 7th 2011

CLOSING BIG DEALS LIFTS YOU HIGH

This is a fast-paced month when things happen quickly. If you're bursting with energy you can get a lot done, but watch you don't overdo things and burn out. It is easy to get carried away when everything is happening so fast. Go with the flow. You have heaven luck on your side and this gets magnified this month. If things proceed smoothly, view this as a sign that you're marching down the right path. If there are too many obstacles, don't keep fighting them in an effort to overcome them. It could be signposts in the wind urging you in a different direction. Listen to your instincts and your inner voice. Don't let things get overcomplicated or you'll wear yourself down. Enjoy the month and take what comes with a positive attitude and a lot of success can be yours this month. For those in business, these are exciting times when big deals can be struck. Here again, if something feels right, it probably is.

WORK & CAREER - *Professional Overdrive*

You're on professional overdrive! You can see the light at the end of the tunnel and your immediate goals are both obvious to you and achievable. In your effort to do more than you should, you could succumb to falling sick. Don't push yourself over the limit. Know when to take a step back and slow down, or you could miss out on valuable productive time stuck in bed. Lack of sleep can lead to lack of concentration at work, leading to careless mistakes. It is more important to stay fresh and keep a clear head this month than to relentlessly slog on through endless hours. Focus on quality not quantity. There may be stress brought on by rivalry at work; competitive co-workers could be egging your subconscious on to do more than you should. Always remember to pace yourself if you want to come out ahead this month.

BUSINESS – *High Profile*

A high-profile month awaits the Snake in business. There is a lot happening and you will find a lot of outside interest in what you're doing. This is a good month to direct more energy to marketing efforts. Think through your strategy carefully. Your image is more important than ever right now because people stop to take notice. Whether it's a good or bad image you project, people will tend to remember this month. Make sure you use this period of prominence to your advantage. When it comes to your finances, keep a closer watch, as your penchant to overspend may spill over to business matters this month. Even if there are exciting deals to pursue, be moderate until you know all eventualities. You can take some risks, but don't put all your eggs in one basket.

LOVE & RELATIONSHIPS - *Pulsating*

Passion pulsates for the Snake person this month. You're alluring and charming to a fault, and others idolize and adore you. This could attract some overzealous admirers into your life. While this is on the one hand flattering, it could become uncomfortable and even intimidating if you a particular someone develops an unwanted infatuation with you. Be polite, but don't let unknown quantities into your inner life so easily. Make friends and accommodate advances, but be careful not to lead anyone on, or there you have the potential to create a monster.

EDUCATION - *Popular*

There's so much happening that the young Snake could find it difficult to concentrate when it comes to studies. To help your concentration levels, get yourself a personalized quartz crystal, and hold it whenever you're trying to study. Before you start to use it, soak it for 7 days and 7 nights in rock salt water; this will cleanse your crystal of other people's energies, allowing your efforts to be stored in it and magnified.

9TH MONTH
Oct 8th - Nov 6th 2011

AUSPICIOUS LUCK KEEPS YOU ALOFT

You're blessed by the wealth star this month. Together with the heavenly star, this boosts business and prosperity luck, allowing you to go ahead with investment and expansion plans with confidence. This is one of your luckiest months this year, so this is the best time to schedule important events in your life. An auspicious time for starting a new business, launching a new initiative, getting married, moving house and entering into new agreements and partnerships. Use this time to pursue your dreams and go for what you want. Enhance this luck further by placing a wishfulfilling jewel in your sector the Southeast; get one for each meaningful wish you make, then watch real magic happen for you.

WORK & CAREER - *Smooth & Trouble-free*

Working life is smooth and trouble free this month. You find it easy to get others on your side, and working in a team situation becomes a real joy because everyone seems to agree with you. You're in a good mood and can expect some happy news in the near future. You may find yourself becoming more money-minded right now, but this will only add to your determination, helping you when it comes to going after that promotion. While others may start to expect a lot from you as your performance improves, don't put undue pressure on yourself. Achieving spectacular results may raise the bar, but as your standards get higher, so will your enthusiasm for the job. Enjoy this month and make the most of it.

BUSINESS - *Superlative*

This promises to be an excellent for business. You have the upper hand in negotiations and others take to you instantly. Many opportunities open up and you are spoilt for choice over which ones to pursue. You cannot cash in on everything, but choose carefully and there is so much potential for a lot of success. You enjoy super growth luck and things you nurture now will bear fruit in the months to come. If there is anything you've been wanting to change, operationally or strategically, this is an opportune time to do so. When making any major changes in direction, always try to do so in a month when your luck is favorable. This month your fortunes are not just favorable, they are superlative. Don't be overly cautious when making decisions. Let your instincts take over a little. Go with the flow and you may just get your big break this month.

LOVE & RELATIONSHIPS - *Magnificent*

You can look forward to a sublime time when it comes to your love life! The Snake person is already an intriguingly beguiling creature, but this month you're simply irresistible! If you mean to have someone, you'll get them. Go after what you want. If your usual style in love is a little laid back, this is the time to seize the bull by the horns and go after what you want with stronger will and determination.

Don't be self-deprecating and don't doubt your own appeal. The more confident you are, the more alluring you become to potential partners. Those of you who are married will find your capacity for love expanding this month. Focus some attention to your marriage and it can be like a second honeymoon for some of you! A good time to rekindling tired romances.

EDUCATION - *Results Come Quickly*

This is a great month for learning. Continue to work hard and you will see results come quickly. Aim high and don't doubt yourself one bit. The more you try, the more you're rewarded. Motivation and drive is easy to come by, so use it to good effect by focusing enough attention on your studies.

10TH MONTH
Nov 7th - Dec 6th 2011

SUCCESSFULLY AVOIDING BAD PEOPLE

While the violent star 7 enters your sector causing some worry in your life, you still enjoy the influence and blessings of the heaven star, nullifying some of the negatives in your life. If things go wrong now and again, look on it as crossing barriers and overcoming hurdles. While there is potential of getting cheated and losing money this month, if you take the necessary precautions, you can successfully avoid getting hit badly. Minimize all risks when it comes to money and personal safety. Don't overexpose yourself when it comes to finances. Conserve rather than splash out. Be careful not to trust anyone too easily. Avoid signing deals and entering into new agreements. Lady Snakes should carry the **Nightspot Protection amulet** this month, and wear a **mantra ring** or some other piece of jewellery featuring sacred mantras; the idea is so you can keep the mantra in contact with your body at all times.

The Snake person should wear a **mantra ring** or some sort of protection this month.

WORK & CAREER - *Keep a Low Profile*

Try to keep a low profile at work this month. Avoid lengthy discussions where the chance of a disagreement could crop up. This is not a time to be controversial. You need allies this month, so nurture your friendships in the workplace. Try not to ruffle any feathers as this could be your undoing. Continue working hard or your slacking will tend to be noticed immediately. There is some danger of being played out, so watch what you say and who you say it to. It is better to play your cards close to your chest when luck is unstable. Ride out the month staying low key, but don't let yourself get disheartened if you hit a snag or two. Things improve next month, so hang in there.

BUSINESS - *Formulate Strategy*

You've been doing so well the last few months that when things hit a few bumps, it may come as a shock to your system. Take any difficulties in your stride. Confronting your problems with the right attitude makes overcoming them much easier for you. Be more careful with money this month. While there may be some good market prospects out there, it is better to wait till next month before making major decisions involving large sums of money. Use this as a time to strategize, but leave the implementation till next month.

LOVE & RELATIONSHIPS – *Tread Carefully*

A dangerous month when it comes to relationships. Married Snakes need to be careful of outsiders who can make trouble for you in your marriage. Even the strongest of unions can be shaken when one of you has your head turned. This month there is a very real risk of that. Wear the **Rooster with Amethyst and Fan** amulet to guard against third party interference. Single Snakes - beware of getting caught in a love triangle. Jealousy may manifest in a perilous form, and when it involves matters of the heart, it can be unexpectedly fierce. Not a good month when it comes to love relationships. Tread carefully.

EDUCATION – *Confide In Your Family*

Pay closer attention to detail this month. Double check your work. It is easy to make careless mistakes when your mind is elsewhere. Get enough rest and try to keep your studies separate from your social life. If there's something weighing on your mind, it might help to talk about it. Confide in someone you can trust, like your parents. Be wary of strangers and "*friends*" you don't know so well. They could betray your trust when you tell them something in confidence.

11TH MONTH
Dec 7th - Jan 5th 2012

MENTOR LUCK GIVES CAREER A BIG BOOST

A good month for the career Snake. Those of you lucky enough to have a mentor figure in your life benefit the most. This is a month full of opportunities; you don't have to look for them, they are right there in front of you! You just need to open your eyes and keep an open mind. Obstacles to success dissolve making your life a lot smoother, easier and happier. Your connections to others play a big role in your life at the moment, helping you achieve what you set out to accomplish. You may need to call on a favor or two. Don't hesitate to pick up the phone if you have to. If you ask, you're unlikely to be turned down, and even if you are, what have you to lose? At least you tried.

WORK & CAREER - *Making An Impression*

You could make a big impression on someone who really matters this month. It could be your direct boss, or someone else in a position of influence or power. The positive results of this may not manifest immediately, but the seeds will have been sown.

Someone more senior than you may take you under their wing; and this person could grow to become a very important part of your professional life later on. You may be invited to join special project meetings. Embrace the opportunity to work closer with top management and do as much as you can to learn.

BUSINESS – *Lucrative*

An extremely lucrative month with opportunities everywhere you look! And within easy reach! This is a month when you feel really hands on in the operational details of what you are doing. You also have excellent charm and interpersonal skills right now, so put them to good use. Other people will tend to fall in line with your judgment, so you happily enjoy holding the upper hand when it comes to discussions and negotiations. Maintain a quiet confidence and you will do extremely well this month. If you have the backing of someone influential, they become exceptionally important right now.

LOVE & RELATIONSHIPS – *Long Term*

There is plenty of love luck for the Snake this month. This is a time to strengthen existing partnerships, or if you are single, watch for the exciting beginnings of a new relationship. Your love life will be more about the long term than short term right now. You will find light-hearted flirting rather innocuous, preferring some form of commitment from your partner. But once you find someone who thinks the way you do, there will be plenty of passion and excitement in your union. Be prepared for relationships that develop out of friendships this month. It may not be love at first sight, but you will feel the heat intensify as you move forward in your feelings for each other.

EDUCATION – *Victory Luck*

You have luck on your side and find yourself very popular with both teachers and classmates. Spending more effort on your studies will reap more than proportionate results. You enjoy good victory luck this month, so anything that pits you against anyone else will see you very competitive, with a real chance of coming out tops. How you do depends on the time and energy you put into the work. Your success this month is not confined to academia. You also do very well in sports and other co-curricular activities. Enjoy the month and make full use of your successes to motivate you to keep doing better and better. Carry a **Victory Banner** or wear a **golden victory key** to boost good luck this month.

12TH MONTH
Jan 6th - Feb 3rd 2012

STAYING ALERT TO MISFORTUNE CHI

You luck nosedives this month with the appearance of several inauspicious stars in your chart. Obstacles arise to hamper the best laid plans. This month it may be better not to make any plans at all, because planning has the maddening effect of resulting in those plans starting to unravel as soon as they are made. This is one of those months where it is better to take each day as it comes. Live life carefully. Avoid taking risks. Think of this as a transitory period. Continue to build on friendships, but don't commit to anything right now. Because you are afflicted by misfortune stars this month, it is necessary to protect yourself with amulets. Display a **five-element pagoda** in the Southeast of your home. Watch your cash flow and try not to overspend.

WORK & CAREER – *Work At Getting Along*

Work may take you on a wild ride in the next few weeks. There may be sudden changes in the people you work with. You may be teamed up with someone you'd rather not work with. But this is not an ideal month to be arrogant. You will be put firmly in your place very quickly. Work to your best ability this month. There may be some indignities to swallow, but you will get your chance for payback another time. While your chart is weak, think about how to get along with everybody rather than how to get ahead of everybody.

BUSINESS – *Conserve Cash*

This is not a good month to take risks or to invest. Delay capital outlays and conserve your cash. Avoid too much publicity this month. It is much better to keep a relatively low profile. Projecting the wrong image now could be damaging for your reputation. Avoid doing deals or signing on anything official this month. While you may meet up with some tempting opportunities, it is best to delay till after February 4th to pursue them. If you miss your chance, let it be. Wanting anything too badly this month could get yourself burnt in the process. You face the monthly Five Yellow, which should be suppressed by wearing a five element pagoda pendant, and countered with a **Tree of Life 5 element pagoda** in the Southeast sector of your office.

Wear the **5 element pagoda** to counter the misfortune energies of the Five Yellow this month.

LOVE & RELATIONSHIPS - *Empathy*

Don't expect too much when it comes to love this month. Your love life consists more of familiar companionship than sizzling hot passion. Right now, what you'll appreciate more in your partner is the ability to empathize and sympathize with you as you go through some difficult and trying times. Looked at this way, if you have a solid relationship with your partner, this could prove to be a satisfying month when you find out how solid your relationship really is.

EDUCATION - *Mildly Overwhelming*

This could be a tiresome time for the young Snake. You may feel slightly overwhelmed by how much you need to get done. Your pals may also be beckoning, and balancing an active social life with a successful academic career could prove more difficult than usual this month. Don't be too hard on yourself. If it's difficult to give your studies your all this month, make a promise to play catch next month. But don't let yourself fall too far behind.

Important Feng Shui Updates for 2011

Part 6

If you have been following the advice given in these Fortune & Feng Shui books on annual feng shui updates, you are already familiar with the time dimension of feng shui which protects against negative luck each year.

This requires overall cleansing and re-energizing of the energy of the home to prepare for the coming of a new year, while simultaneously making placement changes to accommodate a new pattern of chi distribution. Getting rid of old items and replacing with specially made new remedial cures that are in tune with the year's chi brings pristine and fresh new luck into the home.

It is vital to anticipate and quickly suppress the source of malicious chi brought by the new feng shui winds of the year, as this ensures that bad chi originating in afflicted sectors never have a chance to gather, accumulate, grow strong and then ripen in a burst of bad luck! With powerful remedies in place, this will not happen, thereby keeping residents safe from misfortune that can be unsettling and heartbreaking.

Severe bad luck that brings despair can happen to anyone. Sometimes, even in the midst of some personal triumphant moment, your world can suddenly crumble before you. Last year for instance, the world witnessed the incredibly sad falling apart of the marriages of **Kate Winselt** and **Sandra Bullock** soon after they each had reached the pinnacle of their profession by winning the Oscar for Best Actress. Kate had won in 2009 and Sandra in 2010.

Both had gushed and thanked their husbands in their acceptance speeches, obviously unaware of destructive energies lurking within their homes. Both husbands - for whatever reasons - were looking for satisfaction elsewhere outside their marriages! Kate's husband, noted director Sam Mendes' eyes had already started roving in 2009... but the marriage had fallen apart only in 2010 when the grief-bringing star of infidelity made its appearance. Both actresses do not believe in luck... and it is safe to assume they are too busy to have the time to pause, and arrange for the placement of feng shui cures in their homes.

Those not following time dimension feng shui from these books are unlikely to have known that last year 2010 was a year when the external romance star of peach blossom was lurking in every household, creating the potential to cause havoc in marriages! It was vital last year to place cures in the home to protect against outsider third party interference. Sandra Bullock and Kate Winslet are just two of the high profile victims of the star of *External Peach Blossom*! They are exquisitely beautiful ladies, but both of their marriages unraveled in March of 2010!

It is therefore so important that each time we cross into a new year, we should note the particular ailments and afflictions of the year, and then carefully bring in the antidotes so we can sail through the year without having to endure the consequences of bad feng shui, which of course can manifest in different ways. No matter how it manifests, bad luck always brings distress, heartbreak and a sense of helplessness. Why go through this kind of unhappiness when you can prevent or reduce it?

Each year there will be the same kinds of afflictions bringing illness, accidents, robbery, quarrels and severe misfortune, but these afflictions change location each year and vary in strength from year to year. So we need to systematically suppress these *"staples of bad luck"* first.

Then there are the disturbing stars of misfortune - these too need to be neutralized mainly with element therapy so that they do not cast their ill influence onto your luck. In some years, there can be some hazardous or dangerous alignment of energies we need to be careful of, and these also need to be addressed. For instance, we have already told you about the four pillars of clashing elements bringing severe quarrelsome energy that can get violent.

It is so vital for the Snake born to be aware of the potential awaiting them. This is a year when you must be alert to what the *Small* and *Big Auspicious* stars of the 24 mountains bring you. Infusing your home a special aromas can very effectively act as a catalyst for the energies of space and time to fuse seamlessly. Get the special scent infuser and use it to infuse your space with the whiff of good lavender (or other) aromas. Aromas are a powerful way of transcending time and space blending heaven and earth energies to create harmony. In fact, incense and scents, although invisible, are such a powerful way of overcoming obstacles that they have been used by all the major traditions of the world.

> The use of scents and incense is part of spiritual feng shui - the third dimension of inner feng shui - that can make such a difference to really bringing great good fortune into your life.

This is because the right kind of aromas work incredibly well with empowering symbolic placements. Home energy then becomes harmonious and benevolent, blending beautifully with new patterns of chi formations that are flowing through yourhome. Infuse your space with a favorite aroma to feel instantly energized!

Infusing aromas is a powerful way of overcoming obstacles.

Focusing on your house feng shui from this perspective will help you enjoy a better year, irrespective of how good or how bad the indications for the year may be. This is because the correct kind of aromas can go a long way to subduing the afflictions in corners of the house that affect your animal sign, hence protecting you from the affliction of that corner. This also helps strengthen the placement cures that suppress bad feng shui.

Bad luck always have nastier consequences when it catches you unaware. You are sure to feel that you simply cannot cope when you have to face the prospect of losing your job, your home, your good name, your child, your lover or your spouse.

It is only when afflictive energies are effectively suppressed that whatever bad event may occur becomes manageable.

They can even be avoided. This is the wonderful promise and benefit of creating good timely feng shui in the home. And when divine assistance is invoked through the wearing of powerful amulets and sacred talismans, the remedies become even more powerful. This brings harmony and smooth sailing through the year.

Luck is never static. Luck also occurs in cycles, and the key to continuing good fortune is to know when the luck of your house is at its peak and when it requires extra protection. When important areas of the house you live in get hit by misfortune-bringing stars, everyone living within gets hurt.

In the same way, when these same areas are visited by lucky stars, everyone in the house enjoys good luck. To what degree this incidence of good and bad luck affects residents depends also on their personal outlook for the year.

Cycles of luck affect different people in different ways and this is one reason why it can be so beneficial to analyze how the year affects your animal sign. Here we are not just talking about 12 animal signs.

Consider the infinite variations of each individual's pattern of luck when you factor in the two sets of elements in the four sets of birth data - Year, Month, Day and Hour of birth... then factor in the house, the locations of the main door, the bedroom, the dining and living area. Factor in also the changing energies of the year, as well as the energy of the people who surround you, and who make up your circle of family and friends... and you will be awed by the mathematical combinations of chi that are affecting you every single moment!

We cannot take care of everything that affects our luck, but we sure can take care of enough to ensure a pretty good and smooth year. And once we are assured that we have been adequately protected against sudden misfortunes, we can then turn our attention to maximizing and magnifying good fortune for the year... Success, Love, Satisfaction with Life, Money, Wealth, Career highs, Contentment... and a lot more can then be induced to manifest into our lives. This depends on what we want, what we energize for and how we enhance our bedrooms, work spaces and living areas. It is really easier than you think! Just protect against bad luck and energize for good luck.

You must first protect your **main door** and your **bedroom**. Where these two vital spots of your house are located must be protected against bad numbers or bad stars. Afflictive energy can be illness or misfortune numbers, hostile or robbery stars. These can, together with other kinds of negative energy cause loss of some kind.

Someone could force you into litigation - this is something that will happen more often than normal this year; you might suffer perhaps a break up of an important relationship - this too is unfortunately being fanned by the destructive patterns of elements this year. Severe bad luck or loss when it manifests, is always traumatic. Feng shui corrections offer the solutions to avoiding or at least diminishing the chances of negativities happening. Knowing feng shui enables you to anticipate a potentially problematic year; and then to do something about it.

> Correcting and suppressing bad energy is rarely difficult. But it requires a bit of effort.

What you need to do is to systematically go through each of the nine sectors of your home - mentally dividing your home into a three by three sector grid that corresponds to eight compass directions with a center. The next step is to study the year's charts;

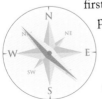

first the Annual Feng Shui chart which pinpoints the afflicted parts of the home, then the 24 mountain charts which show the "*stars*", both lucky and unlucky, that also influence the year's distribution of luck, and finally, the year's four pillars chart. It is the collective and unified analysis of these indications that point to what needs to be done to safeguard the feng shui of any abode.

Suppressing
Flying Star Afflictions for the Year

Traditionally, one of the more important things to update prior to each new year is to find the new locations for all the afflictive star numbers and then to deal with each of them. These yearly afflictions are the same each year, but their strength and severity vary from year to year, depending on where they are. The element of each affliction interacts with the element

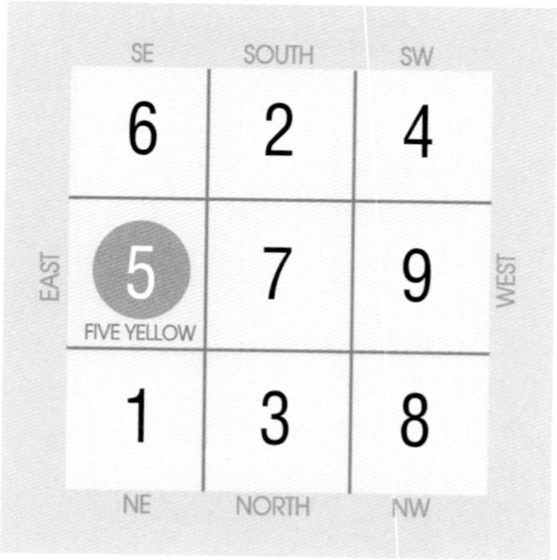

<table>
<tr><td>SE</td><td>SOUTH</td><td>SW</td></tr>
<tr><td>6</td><td>2</td><td>4</td></tr>
<tr><td>5
FIVE YELLOW</td><td>7</td><td>9</td></tr>
<tr><td>1</td><td>3</td><td>8</td></tr>
<tr><td>NE</td><td>NORTH</td><td>NW</td></tr>
</table>

EAST (left side) • WEST (right side)

of the sector they fly into. In some years for instance, the misfortune star number of five yellow a.k.a. **wu wang** can be really strong while in some years they are weaker.

In 2011, the *wu wang* flies to the East, where its Earth element is strongly suppressed by the Wood element here. The 2011 *wu wang* is thus not as strong as it was in the previous year when it occupied the Southwest. There the Earth element of the Southwest strengthened the *wu wang*. In 2011 therefore, we are not so afraid of this otherwise feared star. In spite of this, it is still advisable to keep it under control in case someone in the house is going through weak Life Force year or whose Spirit Essence may be lacking. The Snake's personal chi essence however is very high and has little to fear from the *wu wang*.

Remedies against the Wu Wang

In spite of this, do place traditional remedies to suppress *wu wang* in the East. The *wu wang* is a thoroughly unpleasant star number whose effect could suddenly manifest if your bedroom happens to be here affected by it and it is also being hit by some secret unknown poison arrow, which can act as a catalyst for the wu wang to erupt; or when the Wood element here gets inadvertently weakened for whatever reason.

The wu wang blocks success and affects the luck of the eldest son of the family. So to be safe, get the cures that have been specially designed for the year and place these in the East sectors.

Do not forget the East walls of your important rooms and also the living and family areas where you and your family spend a great deal of time. Place the cures on a sideboard or table, not on the floor!

Five Element Pagoda with Tree of Life

In 2011, we are recommending the five element pagoda that comes with a wood base and is decorated with an all-powerful Tree of Life that grows from the base of the pagoda right to the tip. There are three pairs of birds on the branches of the tree of life. These birds bring opportunities from the cosmic constellations and legend has it they attract exactly the kind of luck a household needs. From the leaves of the tree hang glittering jewels which signify the treasures of the earth, the element that symbolizes wealth and prosperity in 2011. This powerful five element pagoda is actually a transforming tool which turns the all-powerful *wu wang* into a wealth-enhancing tool. Note that this powerful pagoda synchronizes extremely well with the energies of 2011 and 2012 when the *wu wang* flies to the Wood sectors of the compass. It is usually not used during other years.

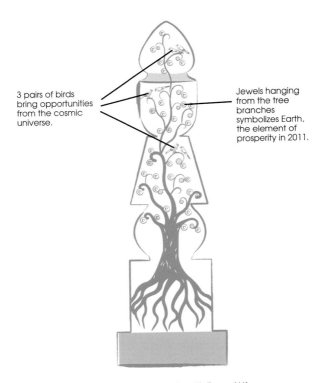

3 pairs of birds bring opportunities from the cosmic universe.

Jewels hanging from the tree branches symbolizes Earth, the element of prosperity in 2011.

The **five element pagoda** with Tree of Life transforms the wu wang into a wealth-bringing star in 2011.

Metal Bell with Tree of Life

Another very beneficial cure for the 2011 wu wang is the powerful Bell which is also made of metal but has a wooden mallet so the sound created is mellower and lower than that of an all-metal bell. The handle of the bell is made of wood; and on the bell itself there is again the amazing tree of life to strengthen the wood chi of the East; and the tree also has 6 birds on its branches; and with jewels on its leaves to signify wealth luck.

This transforms the five element bell into an empowering, enhancing tool which, even as it suppresses the wu wang, is simultaneously sending out powerful vibrations each time the sounds of the bell are created. This way the bell utilizes the wu wang to attract great good fortune opportunities and it is by placing a tree of life with 6 birds that gives it these attributes. We have also embossed the *Dependent Arising mantra* onto both the **five element bell** and **pagoda**.

The **Metal Bell with wooden handle** is another enhancing tool that simultaneously suppresses the wu wang.

This powerful mantra greatly empowers these cures! Those wanting to wear these powerful symbols over the two years 2011 and 2012 can consider wearing either the pagoda or the bell with the tree design to safeguard themselves from the wu wang.

The Snake-born directly suffers from the wu wang in April and also in January 2012, when the wu wang flies into your month chart. This is when you are subjected to a double whammy of bad luck, so do be careful.

Misfortunes caused by the wu wang in 2011 are not as severe as in other years, but they are nonetheless annoying and aggravating. It can cause problems with employees or act as a catalyst for other kinds of bad luck to erupt, so it is a good idea to suppress its negative effect. This year's cure does just that but it also uses the inherent strength of the wu wang to transform bad luck into something good.

If you reside in a room located in the East sector of your house, place the pagoda inside your bedroom. Make sure it is in place before February 3rd which is the start of the lunar new year 2011. It is also important to take note that there should not be any renovations done in the East side of the house through 2011. Avoid all kinds of demolition or digging work although there are some feng shui masters who say that building works are not harmful, arguing that anything productive will not harm the household. We disagree as the wu wang should not be activated by any kind of building. This only strengthens it.

Planting a tree in the East is however very auspicious, especially if you do this on **February 4th**, the day of the **lap chun**!

Other Afflictions of the 2011 Chart

The illness causing star flies to the South in 2011. This is an Earth element star flying into a Fire sector, so here, the illness star gets considerably strengthened, making it a serious threat to residents, but especially for anyone residing in the South sector of the house; but the illness star affects everyone if it is where the main door into the house is located.

Any house that faces or sits South will find that residents within are more vulnerable to catching viruses and falling ill more easily. Try using another door to enter and leave the house by, to avoid over-activating the South.

Should the main door of the house be in the South, the constant opening and closing of the door will energize the star making it more likely to bring illness into the house and this is pronounced during the months of March and December when the month stars mirror that of the year hence bringing a double whammy to afflicted sectors. If your door is facing South, it is a good idea to use another door located in another sector (if possible) especially during these two months. If this is not possible then it is necessary to exhaust the Earth element of the illness star placing something metallic or made of wood here. It is necessary also to remove all Earth element items such as crystals, porcelain vases or stone objects. Also keep lights in the South dim to reduce Fire element energy.

Cures for the Illness Star of 2011

Over the years, we have found that the best way to suppress illness energy brought by the intangible flying star 2 is to suppress its negative effect with a wu lou shaped container made of metal - either in brass or steel. To the Chinese, the wu lou is a container for keeping herbal cures, so that over the years it has come to signify medicinal qualities. Many of China's favorite deities and especially the **Goddess of Mercy**, Kuan Yin are usually depicted carrying a small wu lou shaped little bottle that is said to contain healing nectar.

Placing a large **wu lou** in the South generates invisible healing energies for both physical as well as mental afflictions. It is as good as medicine, and in fact, it is also a very good idea to place a small wu lou by your bedside so that it exudes healing energies even as you sleep. This is good feng shui!

The **Wu Lou with Antahkarana** is a good antidote to falling victim to the Illness Star in the South.

	SE	SOUTH	SW
	6	2 ILLNESS STAR	4
EAST	5	7	9	WEST
	1	3	8
	NE	NORTH	NW

You can also invoke the help of the powerful healing Buddha, also known as the **Medicine Buddha**. This is the blue-bodied Buddha whose image and mantra create so many blessings that the residents of any home that displays the Medicine Buddha image in any way at all, especially in the sector where the illness flying star is located, ill enjoy good health, rarely if ever falling sick.

It is a good idea in 2011 to have an image of **Medicine Buddha** placed on a table top in the **North** part of any room where you spend a great deal of time.

Those feeling poorly in 2011 should also wear **Medicine Buddha bracelets** or our specially designed **moving mantra watches** - the only watches of its kind in the world! We brought out the first such moving mantra watch last year and they have since helped so many people that we have extended our range to include a watch with the healing image of the Medicine Buddha. Wearing such a watch is like having prayers being constantly recited for your good health. It is truly amazing how far technology has progressed. To us, it makes sense to utilize all the technical advances that have made so many wonderful new products possible. Many of the advances in technology have made feng shui very easy to practice.

Wear the **watch** with the healing image of **Medicine Buddha** to improve health and to ward off sickness & disease.

The Quarrelsome Hostile Star flies to the North in 2011

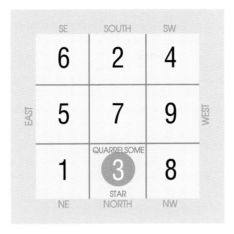

This is a Wood element star flying into a Water element sector. As such, this noisy, litigation-bringing star number is both strong and harder to overcome. It is dangerous and aggravating and very capable of causing anyone staying in the North sector a great deal of problems. This is the major affliction affecting anyone having a bedroom in the North sector in 2011.

You are likely to be more easily stressed out and this will affect your productivity levels. For some, it can even create obstacles that block your luck. At its worst, the effect of this affliction is to be hit with someone bringing you into litigation, causing you no end of aggravating pressure and inconveniences, or someone getting violent with you.

This star brings an pervasive feeling of hostility, short tolerance levels and a great deal of impatience. There will be arguments, fights and misunderstandings for everyone directly hit by it. Unfortunately for anyone having a bedroom in the North sector of the house, the quarrelsome star 3 is made stronger this year because its Wood Element is produced even more by the Water element of the North.

As a Wood element star, the best way to subdue its effect is to exhaust it with Fire Element energy. Anything that suggests Fire is an excellent cure, so bright lights and the color red are excellent remedies. Hence, because the North is associated with water energy, the danger is enhanced so remedying it is vital.

An excellent cure against the 3 star is the **Red Dragon amulet**. This brings luck while keeping the number 3 star subdued. It is excellent for anyone having their bedroom in the North or has doors that face North.

Note that this amulet has the Dragon carrying a sword in its right claw as this helps overcome all the clashing elements of the year.

An excellent amulet for the Snake to carry in 2011 is the **Red Dragon Amulet**. This brings good luck to the Snake while keeping any quarrelsome energies in check.

The Violent Star 7
attracts bad people into the home

The Violent Star 7 which attracts bad people into the home is in the center of the chart this year, where it is symbolically locked up, hence reducing its influence. This is an affliction which hurts most when it occupies one of the outer sectors of any building, but trapped in the center, its negative impact is less severe. The number 7 star number is an Metal element number and with the center being an Earth sector, here we have a situation of Earth producing Metal, so while it may be hemmed in in the center, it is nevertheless troublesome. It is a number that causes loss through being cheated or robbed.

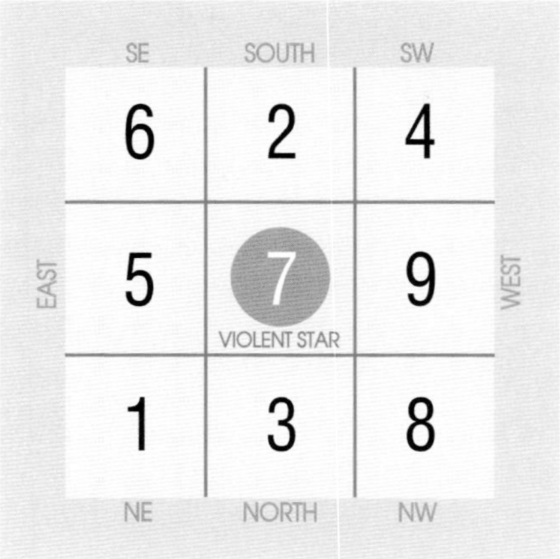

SE	SOUTH	SW
6	2	4
5	7 VIOLENT STAR	9
1	3	8
NE	NORTH	NW

EAST (left side) · WEST (right side)

A good way of keeping this affliction under wraps is simply to place a small sideboard in the center of the house, place seven pieces of metal within and then lock it up. This symbolically "*locks up*" the number 7 star very effectively. At the same time, have **a Rhino with an Elephant** near the entrance into the home.

However, should any of you be feeling vulnerable with the burglary star in the center of the home, you can safeguard yourself by carrying the **blue-colored Rhino and Elephant** or using it as a hanging on your bags or hung in the car. It is good practice to stay protected against encountering bad people who would want to harm you. Use the **Blue Rhino and Elephant protector** as this continues to be an effective cure in 2011. It is a highly respected cure against the potential violence of the 7.

Carry **a blue-colored Rhino and Elephant hanging** to stay protected against encountering bad people and those who do not have your best interests at heart.

Note that the problem with the number 7 star in 2011 is that being in the center of the feng shui chart, the number 7 can potentially spread its influence into any part of the house, hence it is necessary to keep it well under control.

The best is to literally *"lock it up"*, otherwise it simply plays havoc with house security. It is very inconvenient and even dangerous when the 7 star number strikes.

In 2011
the God of the Year cannot be ignored

The Tai Sui is important because this year it directly faces the *Star of Natural Disaster* in the West. This is a 24 mountain star that sits between the two stars of *three killings*! That there are such intensive negative stars directly confronting the Tai Sui is not good for the year. It suggests a battle, and when a battle takes place, there is always collateral damage! Especially when they are read against the background of the year's clashing elements in the four pillars; these signs collectively indicate clear and present danger.

How the dangers of the year manifest will vary in timing and severity for different houses and different countries; but generally, an afflicted Tai Sui means that the wars of the world currently being waged on several fronts are unlikely to decline. There is also no let up in the occurrence of natural disasters.

Do be extra mindful of the Tai Sui in 2011. Avoid confronting it. Avoid facing East and make extra efforts not to "*disturb*" its location, the East sector of the house.

This sector must be kept quiet as noise activates the Tai Sui and incurs its wrath. Also avoid digging, banging or renovating this side of the home.

It is beneficial to place a well-executed art piece of the beautiful Pi Yao in the East as this celestial creature is excellent for appeasing the Tai Sui. The Pi Yao always brings good feng shui and it is for this reason that you will find many artistic variations of this auspicious creature all over China and Hong Kong. It is a great favorite with people who believe in feng shui. It brings exceptional good fortune into the home.

For 2011, a Pi Yao made in Earth element material is preferred as this element signifies wealth luck. So crystal or ceramic Pi Yao, or one made in liu li medium, would be excellent.

Place a **Pi Yao** in the East sector of the home this year to appease the Tai Sui who resides there in 2011.

It is important for everyone whose bedroom is in the **East,** or whose sitting direction while working is facing or sitting East, to place the **Pi Yao** near you.

It does not matter if the Pi Yao is standing or sitting but it should appear proud and majestic looking. The more beautiful looking the Pi Yao is the better it is to display in the house to appease the Tai Sui. This advice applies to anyone irrespective of their animal sign. The place of the Tai Sui is taken very seriously in feng shui. It is emphasized in the *Treatise on Harmonizing Times and Distinguishing Directions* compiled under the patronage of the Qianlong Emperor during his reign in the mid-Eighteenth century and any Master practicing feng shui in China or Hong Kong always ensures the Tai Sui is respected and thus taken account of in their updating process.

The Emperor Qiang Lung inspired Treatise states that the locations where the Tai Sui resides and where the Tai Sui has just vacated are lucky locations. So note that in 2011, the locations of East and NE1 are considered lucky benefiting from the lingering energy of the Tai Sui. Those having their rooms in these two locations will enjoy the patronage and protection of the Tai Sui in 2011. The Treatise further explains that it is unlucky to reside in the location where the Tai Sui is progressing towards i.e. clockwise on the astrology compass. In 2011 this means the Southeast 1 location; it is unlucky to directly confront the Tai Sui's residence. It is unlucky to "*face*" the Tai Sui because this is deemed rude, so the advice for 2011 is to not to directly face East.

Tai Sui Amulet to subdue the Grand Duke
Jupiter for the year 2011.

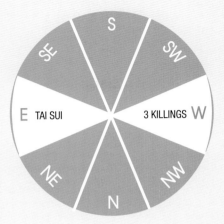

In 2011, never forget to avoid confronting the Tai Sui. **Do not face East this year** even if this is your success direction under the Kua formula of personalized lucky directions.

Those who forget and inadvertently face the Tai Sui run the risk of offending the Tai Sui. This brings obstacles to your work life. Your road to achieving success gets constantly interrupted and for some, supporters can turn into adversaries.

In 2011, the West of every building is afflicted by the Three Killings

This affliction brings three severe misfortunes associated with loss, grief and sadness. Its location each year is charted according to the animal sign that rules the year. Thus in 2011 it flies to the West because the Rabbit belongs to the Triangle of Affinity made up of the Rabbit, Sheep and Boar; with the Rabbit occupying a cardinal direction (East).

The Three Killings is thus in the West, the direction that is directly opposite the Rabbit. This feng shui

aggravation affects only primary directions, so unlike other feng shui afflictions, the direct bad effects of the *three killings* are felt over a larger area of the house. When you suffer a sudden reversal of fortune, it is usually due to being hit by the three killings.

In 2011 the *three killings* resides in the West, where it poses some danger to the young daughters of the family. Anyone occupying the West would be vulnerable to being hit by the *three killings*. For everyone whose bedroom and/or main doors face West or are located in the West sector of your home, please get the celestial protectors - the Chi Lin, the Fu Dog and the Pi Yao - preferably made colorful and with a fierce expression.

For them to be effective, some texts refer to the three different deities traditionally seated on their backs, but as a feng shui cure, they are as effective on their own, although the secret is to make sure they have their different implements with them as these enable them to overcome the afflictions. Thus the **Sword** on the back of the **Pi Yao** protects against loss of wealth. The **Lasso** on the back of the **Chi Lin** protects against loss of loved one. The **steel hook** on the back of the **Fu Dog** protects against loss of good name. The hook is a very powerful implement which also "*hooks in wealth luck*".

Do not use antique images as feng shui cures as these are usually surrounded by tired chi. It is important that feng shui remedies have fresh energy so there is strong vigor and vitality chi attached to them. Antique furniture decorated with celestials can be lovely to look at, but they rarely make powerful cures. They can however generate auspicious chi after they are cleansed of lingering yin vibes.

Use a dry cloth with sea salt or crystal salt to wipe off stale chi. Do this cleansing ritual at least once a year. The month before the lunar new year is a good time. The energy of the *three killings* can sometimes stick onto furniture, especially those that have animals or human images painted onto them. It is a good idea to use raw salt as a way of wiping off lingering bad chi.

Display the **3 celestial protectors** in the West to counter the 3 Killings affliction in 2011. It is even better when these protectors carry the implements of the Deities they are associated with, as these enable them to effectively overcome the afflictions.

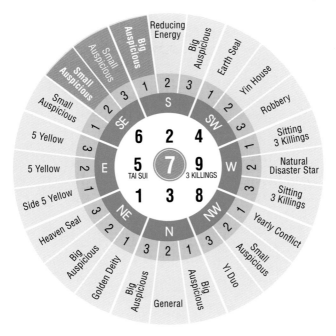

The Snake's SE3 location is flanked by Small
Auspicious and Big Auspicious in 2011.

Those of who may want to
stay protected from the *three killings* and
prevent them from overwhelming you when
you are out and about this year can also
hang the **three celestials amulet** on your
handbags and pocket books.

Those of you staying in the West sectors of the house
could experience bad dreams and if so, make sure you
place the **three celestial guardians** on a cabinet along
the West wall of the room. If you have a window in
the bedroom, place the three celestials
there even if it is not the West wall. The
presence of the three guardians is a
powerful cosmic force that protects.

Carry the **3 Celestial Guardian
with Implements Keychain** to
protect against the 3 Killings.

Strengthening
Left & Right of Snake's Luck

The Snake benefits from the stars of the 24 mountains in 2011 as this circle of cosmic energy brings two lucky stars, the *Small Auspicious* on the Snake's left and the *Big Auspicious* on the Snake's right. In addition the Snake is itself sitting on the star of *Small Auspicious* in the SE3 location of the compass zodiac. This is really auspicious. To activate these very lucky stars, do create a water feature in the SE 2, SE 3 and South 1 - the three sectors occupying 45 degrees of space in this part of your house of garden. Creating the physical presence of water here will attract great wealth luck. Besides there is also something big coming your way and it will likely happen in October of the year.

So the year 2011 is a wonderful opportunity to tap into your lucky stars by installing a large water feature in the South 1 and Southeast 2/3 sectors of your garden or living area of the house. The water features do not need to be big, but the presence of moving water here is very beneficial for anyone born in the year of the Snake. The SE sector especially benefits from the presence of water as this is also the symbolic location for asset accumulation but in 2011, the SE also has the powerful heavenly star 6. It is important to get the location right, so do take your compass directions carefully.

If you find it difficult to install real water features which has a pump that creates yang water, then placing a table with a pair of brass urns filled with water here is also good. This is creating water that is yin, but it is as effective because the three stars here are both yin and yang. Change the water in the urn daily and make sure they are always in the correct location.

Placement feng shui works best when there is accuracy of compass readings so it is a good idea to invest in a good compass and to learn to take accurate compass readings.

Enhancing Snake's Awesome Luck

In 2011 the Snake needs to use the heavenly seal in all its correspondence as this is a year when heaven luck brings great good fortune to the Snake. The Snake enjoys a combination of astrological indications of good things coming to fruition. There are many good ideas and offers making their way to you so you need to ensure correct feng shui is in place. Symbols of good fortune should be placed in your Snake location of SE3. A few of these are suggested here for you to see which are those you can find to invite into your home.

The sailing ship bringing gold is a powerful symbol of success and is a great favorite with the Chinese tycoons of Asia and in fact there are dynastic fortunes founded at the turn of the twentieth century using the sailing ship as their logo with great success. The sailing ship brings wealth from the winds and waters… Place a few ships stacked with gold ingots sailing into your direction to energize for good luck.

Meanwhile, to assuage any feelings of envy sent your way by people with the evil eye, you can also get the antidote against the evil eye which is an eye in a circle made in blue, white and turquoise and then hang this anywhere high near you or on a tall tree outside your house. The anti evil eye hangings are so powerful that many countries around the Mediterranean sea hang it and wear it all year around their necks, to push away all harm brought by envious eyes. It is always good to stay protected against the evil eye because you never know who or why anyone would want to feel envious of you. You can also wear the protection which we have made into a scarf that powerfully pushes such bad people away from you.

Let a **sailing ship** laden with treasures sail into the SE, the Snake direction, to bring you success and wealth.

Scents to Transcend
the Cosmic Fields of Energy

Aromas such as lavender can be used to transcend the cosmic fields of energy that surround us. We have spent the past year talking about the third dimension of feng shui, and the use of aromas is one of the more common ways used by Masters skilled in the shamanistic aspects of feng shui practice. At its most basic, joss sticks are used during the Wealth God welcoming rituals performed during the night before the Lunar New Year; during such rituals, strong smells such as sandalwood are used. These cut through the energy of space connecting heaven with earth chi.

Scents are a powerful medium for clearing the air of negatives and to suppress troublesome energies that bring aggravations. Aromas are associated with the transcendence of chi energy between cosmic realms of consciousness and are an advanced form of practice used in the old days by expert practitioners. All afflictions can be dissolved with ritualistic incense pujas; and there are other aromatic pujas that can manifest good fortune.

An excellent way to energize the 6 star is to utilize celebration aromas, and in the case of the Snake, what is needed is sandalwood incense OR simple calming lavender oils which, when infused into the atmosphere can be extremely beneficial. This can either be sprayed into the Southeast of the living area or they can be infused into the air. Do this by placing a few drops of the aroma oil onto a small dish containing water that is kept warm with a tea light. A few minutes is all it takes to infuse the air with the aroma. Do this once a week on a day that is lucky for you or on a day when you have a special meeting scheduled. You can also do it daily if you wish. After a week or so, you find that there will always be hint of good aromas in the air.

Activating the Trinity of Tien Ti Ren

In the year 2011, **all four primary directional locations** - North, South, East and West - are afflicted, as we have seen with the *Illness*, *Hostile*, *Five Yellow* and *Natural Disaster* star. Of the four, only the West location has the lucky 9 star number, but 9 in a Metal element sector always contains hidden dangers; so correcting and placing remedies to safeguard the cardinal locations of the house is extremely important in 2011.

The **four secondary directions** on the other hand, are indicating extremely lucky star numbers, with 8 leading the way as it flies into the patriarchal corner of Northwest, followed by the heavenly 6 in the opposite direction of Southeast. Then there is the victory star in the Northeast and the star of romance and scholarship in the Southwest in 2011.

With this kind of star number configurations, we also note that the Northeast/Southwest axis (which is the favorable axis of this current period of 8) has been blessed with the star of earth seal in the SW and the matching counterpart star of the *Heaven Seal* in the Northeast. The presence of these heaven and earth stars are indicative of the need for the trinity of lucky cosmic forces to be present in the North and the South, the other set of axis directions which are showing a set of two *Big Auspicious* stars. In N1 and N3 and also in S1 and S3, we see here a quartet of important lucky stars brought by the circle of the 24 mountains.

In 2011, there is the strong indication of substantial changes taking place in the world which will **bring benefits to some** and **loss to others**. This is vital to understand, as the year itself is showing a set of four pillars which not only has **4 sets of clashing elements** but also **two yang and two yin pillars**. This suggests that the complementarily of cosmic forces is balanced. **Yin and yang are in balance**.

Good fortune manifests as growth, sudden windfalls and big transformations of luck that bring a "*house filled with jewels*" enabling one to "*wear the jade belt*" if the household successfully activates the trinity of *Tien Ti Ren*. In other words, there must be plentiful supply of heaven, earth and mankind energies! This is something that is beneficial to ensure at all times, but more so in 2011, when severe bad luck indications are balanced against equally powerful auspicious indications. So the important thing is to tap into the positive energies of the year, thereby getting onto the growth spiral. *Tien ti ren* is the key! Symbolically, just placing the words heaven and earth is often good enough to complement the presence of people within a home.

Mankind chi is the powerful yang chi that activates the yin earth chi and the cosmic heaven chi.

In the old days, wealthy households would always include miniature mountains to signify Earth, and also all the Deities of their faith - Taoism or Buddhism, the **8 Immortals** and the **18 Holy Beings** - all to signify heaven chi while at the same time imbuing their homes with activity and celebrations to signify mankind chi. This infusion of yang energy acts a catalyst to generate the presence of the powerful cosmic trinity.

In this way did wealthy households of the past live, and over the years, these practices came to signify the cultural underpinnings of the Chinese way of life. Thus one should not be surprised to note that many Chinese households believe that the blessing power of heaven is brought in by the presence of deities on their family altar. The family altar was always placed rather grandly, directly facing the front door. This signified the continuing presence of heaven luck. It was important to keep the family altars clean with offerings of food, lights, water, wine and incense made daily.

Wealthier households would even have professionals such as monks and holy men, who would come and recite prayers for the family at special dates in the year. These were daily rituals believed to keep the family patriarch safe and the household in a state of abundance. In other words, keeping their lifestyles secure.

In addition, good Earth chi was assured by the presence of mountains and rivers simulated in landscaped gardens around the home and symbolized by **mountain scenery paintings** inside the home.

Good feng shui also ensures good chi flows through the rooms and corridors of the house.

Finally, excellent mankind chi is kept flowing fresh and revitalizing yang energy. **Auspicious phrases** and lucky rhyming couplets were placed as **artistic calligraphy** in important rooms of the house; this was the equivalent of today's very popular "*affirmation*s".

The Chinese have been living with these powerful affirmations for as long as anyone can remember, and there are literally thousands of such lucky phrases such as "*your wealth has arrived*" or "your luck is as long as the yellow river"... and so forth. These are popular sayings exchanged between families during festive seasons and during Chinese New Year. Anyone wanting to enjoy good fortune continuously must be mindful of the power generated by *tien ti ren* chi inside their homes. This is very timely for 2011 to help you benefit from the year.

In 2011 therefore, the three dimensions of feng shui - space and time as well as the dimension which engages the cosmic force within the self (the purest source of yang energy generated from within you) must all be present. In fact, this is a major secret of feng shui. This is the mankind chi that pulls heaven and earth chi together. Good mankind chi requires you to stay positive, to generate lucky aspirations and to anticipate good outcomes. Your expectations must be high. You can enhance the empowerment of your own self. This unlocks for you the strength of mankind luck - *ren* chi - which pulls time and space into a powerful whole. With this kind of attitude, you can then start to enhance the four lucky secondary directions with powerful enhancing placement feng shui:

Enhancing the Chi of 8 in the Northwest

The all-powerful and auspicious 8 flies to the place of the patriarch in 2011, bringing quite exceptional great good fortune to all the father figures of the world.

SE	SOUTH	SW
6	2	4
5	7	9
1	3	8
NE	NORTH	NW

EAST (left side) WEST (right side)

AUSPICIOUS (under 8)

Being located in the Northwest, the 8 Earth Star also gets very considerably strengthened, especially since it is flying to the NW from the center where it was located last year.

As an annual star number, the 8 is indeed very strong. It brings good relationship luck and it brings success and wealth. It is a powerful star at its zenith. What worked last year, the **crystal 8** embedded with real 24 carat gold, continues to work this year, so do display it in the Northwest of the house; or of your office. But the crystal 8 becomes even more powerful when it is placed alongside a **crystal Ru Yi**, the **scepter of authority**. This is especially beneficial for Chief Executive Officers i.e. CEOs and bosses; in fact, anyone in a position of authority and power will benefit from the Ru Yi placed alongside the 8.

In the old days, these symbols were recommended for mandarins at court - equivalent to the Ministers and top business leaders of today. Those who want a boost to their career should consider placing this powerful symbol of advancement and upward mobility in the Northwest corner of their home, office or home office.

Place a **Ru Yi** alongside a **crystal 8** for career strength and longevity.

With the 8 flying into the Northwest, the Ru Yi placed next to the 8 becomes especially effective. Place the Ru Yi in exactly the middle of the NW sector i.e. in NW2, as this is the auspicious part of this location.

Activating the Power of Heavenly 6 in the Southeast

The number 6, a lucky white star usually associated with the cosmic energies of heaven, flies to the Southeast in 2011, directly facing the Northwest, thereby creating a powerful alliance between heaven and earth luck, bringing luck not only to the Southeast but also to the Northwest, directly opposite.

SE	SOUTH	SW
6 HEAVENLY STAR	2	4
5 	7	9
1	3	8
NE	NORTH	NW

There is great synergy luck between father and eldest daughter in the family. Should either the master bedroom or the daughter's bedroom be located in the Southeast, unexpected developments take place that lift the family fortunes higher than ever. The 6 star brings heaven's celestial blessings and good fortune for those blessed by its cosmic chi. This occurs when your bedroom is located in the Southeast; and if so, do make an effort to fill your room with yang chi energy, a higher noise level and perhaps greater movement in your room. In other words, make it vibrate with energy, as this will energize it, acting as a catalyst for good fortune to occur. This brings immediate good fortune to the Snake in 2011 although the good benefits come in a series of good events and good news befalling them rather than in one single good event.

It is an excellent idea to place images of both the **Snake** as well as the **Dragon** in the **Southeast** and to bring additional light into this part of the house or to this corner of your favorite room.

The number 6 signifies authority and power. It is associated with economics and finances. At its peak, 6 stands for authority, influence and control over money. Appearing in the Southeast, it suggests financial management does well under a mature woman. Within the family, the year suggests that money should be handled by women, and power by men. On balance, the male leader has greater strength than the female, but it is the woman who holds the purse strings. This is the way the energies are laid out for the year. Those observing this pattern of energy and flow with it are most likely to benefit from 2011. It is beneficial to bring this auspicious 6 star to life as it really benefits the entire household, especially in houses where the SE is not a tight corner or a small room that locks up its good energy.

To invoke the best kind of results from the 6 star in 2011, display the **Tree of Wealth** in the SE. Hang **6 large coins** from the tree, and if there are also **6 birds** on the tree, it signifies exciting news coming to the household. The best way to create this effect is to find a healthy growing tree and place it in the SE before hanging auspicious symbols that ignite the intrinsic power of 6. Remember, 6 birds and 6 large coins will attract heaven luck.

Display the **Tree of Wealth** in the Southeast in 2011.

Magnifying Victory Luck of 1 in the Northeast

The number 1 star, which brings triumph and success, flies to the Northeast corner in 2011. So anyone who resides in this part of the house benefits from this lucky star number. Anyone living here will feel its benevolent effect, as the number 1 star attracts all kinds of triumphant moments. This kind of luck is especially welcome by those engaged in competitive pursuits, as it helps you win.

In 2011 this star brings winning luck to young men, especially those who are ambitious and keen

SE	SOUTH	SW
6	2	4
5	7	9
1	3	8

EAST / WEST

VICTORY STAR
NE · NORTH · NW

to succeed. What is exciting is that the direction Northeast benefits from three good stars of the 24 mountains, so there is some very exciting potential that can be tapped from this location. It is a good idea to keep the NE energized through the year. Do not let it get too quiet. Yang energy should be created by making sure this part of the house or of your favorite room stays well lit and is occupied. At all costs, prevent *yin spirit formation* by not keeping the sector too silent through the year.

The most auspicious symbols to place here in the NE are all the symbols that signify victory such as awards, certificates, trophies and victory banners. You can also fly a flag in the NE sector this year. The flag always suggests the announcement of victories.

Place a symbol of victory like the
Victory Banner in the NE this year.

Benefiting
from the Star of Scholarship & Romance
in the Southwest

Finally, the fourth lucky secondary location of 2011 is Southwest, which benefits from the romance and scholastic star of 4. This is a very powerful star of love and will bring beautiful romantic energy to anyone residing in the Southwest.

This is, in any case, the location associated with marriage and domestic happiness. It is also the place of the mother, so the matriarchal force is associated with the SW. With the romantic star 4 placed here, all the

SE	SOUTH	SW
6	2	4
EAST 5	7	9 WEST
1	3	8
NE	NORTH	NW

stress and strains associated with the five yellow of the past year has definitely dissolved. In 2011, this location brings love and marriage opportunities. It also brings better harmony and appreciation of the mother figure within families and households.

The number 4 is often associated with romantic peach blossom vibrations, so the luck of this sector directly benefits those still single and unmarried. For those already married, peach blossom brings a happier family life. Domestic energies get enhanced and those who know how to energize the SW with **bright lights** will find the number 4 star will jazz up their love relationships.

Scholastic Luck

Those residing in the Northeast part of the house also benefit from the other influences brought by the number 4 star. These benefits are related to scholastic and literary pursuits, and the star brings good academic luck to those having their bedroom here. Facing Northeast is also beneficial for students and those sitting for examinations.

The direction Northeast stands for wisdom and learning, so this auspicious number is a very positive star here. The only problem will be that love can also be a distraction, so if you want to enhance the scholastic side of this star, you should place literary symbols here.

Anyone involved in a writing or literary career will also benefit from being located in the NE. But do make sure you activate the sector with bright lights. Fire element energy is excellent to add to the strength of the sectors' good luck. Doing so strengthens both the romance as well as the scholastic dimensions of your fortunes in 2011. So light up this corner as best you can!

Magnifying the Earth Element to Enhance Resources

Updating feng shui each year involves more than taking care of lucky and unlucky sectors. It also requires being alert to the balance of elements and their effects on the year's energy flows. This is revealed in the year's four pillars chart which, in 2011 indicates an absence of the Earth element in the primary chart of the year.

The intrinsic element of the year as indicated by the heavenly stem of the **Day Pillar** is yang Metal, and altogether there are three Metal elements in the chart. There are also three Wood elements, one Water and one Fire, making then a total of the eight elements that make up the primary chart of the year.

The Earth element is however missing in 2011, and the Earth element symbolizes resources. This makes Earth **a very important element,** because without resources, none of the other indicated attributes such as wealth, success, prosperity, creativity and so forth can manifest.

This is one of the secrets in Paht Chee reading. It is always important that the intrinsic element (in this year, it is Metal) is kept continually replenished by having the element that produces it present.

In 2011, this means the Earth element, because Earth produces Metal; hence Earth is the resource element for 2011 (do note that this changes from year to year). As Earth is the missing element this year, anyone who makes the effort to magnify the presence of Earth element in their living spaces is bound to enjoy excellent feng shui. And Earth element is best symbolized by either a **picture of mountains** or better yet, having the presence of crystals, stones and rocks which come from within the earth.

This is the key that unlocks the manifestation of other kinds of luck. It is important to create the presence of Earth element objects in the home and to also strengthen the Earth element corners of the home. These are the Southwest and Northeast. Keep these two corners of the home well lit so that the Fire element is ever present to effectively strengthen these Earth element sectors.

The paht chee chart does however show that there is hidden Earth, but here, the Earth element is not immediately available. Nevertheless, it does indicate the availability of hidden resources. When the Earth element gets magnified, the economics of your living situation becomes extremely comfortable.

So do place stones, rocks or crystals - the best are the large circular **crystal globes** - on your coffee table in the living area and then shine a light on it so that the energy of the Earth element gets diffused through the room. Also enhance all compass Earth sectors - Northeast and Southwest as well as the center - in the same way.

Creating a "*mountain*" with rocks or pebbles in an artistic way also brings excellent feng shui potential. Indeed, it is not only the Chinese who have a tradition of creating "*miniature mountains*" in and around their gardens and homes. Many other Eastern traditions where feng shui is popularly practiced - such as Japan and Korea - also have their own artistic recreations of mountain scenery. This always signifies the Earth element.

Create a **mountain of pebbles** in your home to activate the all-important resource element of Earth in 2011. The NE and SW activated this way brings valuable hidden resource luck to the home.

Hidden Earth

We need to look at the entire paht chee chart to highlight the element that is in most short supply; this involves looking at all the elements of the year's chart including the hidden elements. In 2011, there are three elements of hidden Earth, which bring about a magnification of the Earth element. But in expanding the analysis to include the hidden elements, we need to also take note of the shortage of the Water element. So as in the previous year, the Water element continues to be needed.

In this respect, 2011 is better than 2010, because this year there is one Water element available (last year Water was completely missing). The Hour pillar has yang Water as its heavenly stem. But Water needs to be supplemented to keep the elements in good balance.

Adding to the strength of Water strengthens the Wood element for the year and this is beneficial. This is because Wood symbolizes prosperity and financial success. Hence the placement or addition of the Water element in the Wood sectors East and Southeast creates excellent wealth feng shui.

Under the Eight Aspirations formula of feng shui, the Southeast is also the sector that stands for prosperity via the accumulation of wealth. To activate this sector, Water required, but Water without Earth is not as effective as Water with Earth! So what is required is the placement of a **Crystal Water Feature** in the Southeast corner. This would be then an excellent wealth energizer for 2011. Any kind of water presence for this corner in any room that you frequently use (except your bedroom) would be excellent feng shui.

Nine Wealth Gods to Materialize Prosperity Luck

The final feng shui tip we would like to share with readers for the year is the placement of a ship bringing nine wealth gods sailing into your home. This has great relevance for the year as it suggests that the winds and waters will bring the divine personifications of wealth luck into the home.

Wealth Gods are a very effective for symbolic placement in feng shui folklore, and it is for this reason that the Chinese always invite Wealth Deities into the home. But there are certain years when the Wealth gods are especially effective and that is when the *Big Auspicious* stars of the 24 mountains fly into two opposite primary directions, which is the case in 2011. Both the North and the South sectors of every home have, and thus can benefit from these stars; but they work only if they can be energized by the presence of Wealth Deities which are believed to bring good cosmic chi into the homes. This will activate the North-South axis. So do place the ship in a North-South orientation within the home.

Powerful Talismans & Amulets For 2011

Part 7

If you have been following the advice given in these Fortune & Feng Shui books on annual feng shui updates, you are already familiar with the time dimension of feng shui which protects against negative luck each year.

This requires overall cleansing and re-energizing of the energy of the home to prepare for the coming of a new year, while simultaneously making placement changes to accommodate a new pattern of chi distribution. Getting rid of old items and replacing with specially made new remedial cures that are in tune with the year's chi brings pristine and fresh new luck into the home.

This is a fabulously lucky year for the Snake. The annual heaven star makes its way into your chart and you are surrounded by *Big Auspicious* luck on all sides. Your strong Life Force and Spirit Essence means that you not only enjoy good fortune luck, but that you will be strong enough to receive it. Opportunities that come your way can be seized easily, and plans you set in motion have every chance of success. Aim high this year, and carry all the talismans needed to actualize this good fortune luck. Years like this one don't come along all the time, so when you're fortunate enough to enjoy such superlative indications, do try your best to make the most of them.

Attract Opportunity Luck with the Heaven Seal Activator

The Snake person has the auspicious white star number 6 in its sector this year, bringing opportunities from the heavens. Your big break could come along, so keep a look out. Be bold in your aspirations, and be willing to accept help from others. There are a lot of people who are not only willing to help but also able to do so. Activate this kind of luck with the **Heaven Seal Activator**, which features the **Jade Emperor of Heaven** on one side and the **Chien trigram** on the other. This will bring you the luck and the strength you will need to convert good opportunities into truly awesome results.

Use the Enhancing Mirror to Absorb the Power of 8 from the NW

The auspicious number 8 star lies in the Northwest this year, directly opposite your home location, bringing it in direct confrontation with you. Embrace this good fortune by carrying the Enhancing Mirror, which features the Big Auspicious word, surrounded by the sacred syllables *Om Ah Hum*; this will attract and absorb power of 8 energy from the Northwest, allowing you to directly benefit from it.

This mirror also works to deflect away bad luck and the evil intentions of others, something you may have to watch out for. The more successful you get, the more reason you give others to envy you. Transform negative thoughts from others into positive ones, and turn your rivals into supporters with this sacred mirror.

Display the Water Globe with Tree of Life in the Snake's Home Direction

This crystal water globe comes with the Tree of Life and the 4 Dharmakhaya mantras at the bottom. Water is the element that appears to be totally missing from the year's Paht Chee chart, so having this water globe will help redress the balance of energies, allowing you to take full advantage of your positive luck this year. The spherical shape of the globe while ensures smooth and harmonious relationships with family, friends, colleagues and within your marriage. Display this water globe in your animal sign location of Southeast, or in the center of your living room.

Pull in the Luck of Big Auspicious with the Horse with Jewels

Make the most of the luck of Big Auspicious in your chart by displaying a tribute horse entering your home from the Southeast. Let the horse pull in plenty of jewels to signify an abundance of prosperity.

Hang a 6-rod Victory Banner Windchime in the Southeast

The Victory Banner windchime creates the most lovely sound and enhances the number 6 heavenly star in your location of Southeast. Hang this windchime in the Southeast for it to bring you good fortune in abundance as well as unexpected windfall and mentor luck.

Victory in Gambling Talisman Brings Luck when Taking Risks

This talisman features the Windhorse together with its mantra and the Sigil of Jupiter to bring you victory luck in whatever gamble you take. Carry this talisman in your handbag. This will help you if you plan to invest big or plan to take some risks involving money.

Dispel Three Killings Chi with the 3 Celestial Protectors

The three celestial guardians are the best cure for the Three Killings affliction which comes from the West in 2011. Depicted with their implements, the Chi Lin carries the Lasso, the Fu Dog carries the Hook, while the Pi Yao has the Sword. Together these three guardians will dispel the negative energy coming your way from this affliction, protecting against loss of relationships, loss of good name and loss of wealth. Display them in the West part of your living room or home and also in the West of your office.

Make Best Use of Positive Affirmations to Unleash the Power of your Subconscious

Positive words and affirmations when viewed over and over are like mantras that enter your subconscious. This year we have incorporated these affirmative and positive sayings into several of our new items as powerful activators of good luck. Our glass pebbles and mandala stones with positive words and auspicious symbols can be displayed in your animal sign location of Southeast for best effect.

Put them in a pot or bowl in the SE, or even better, load them onto a miniature sailing ship, letting the ship sail in from one of your good directions. You can also add these stones into your mandala offering set.

Powerful Gemstones
to Connect Your Lucky Day
with the Seven Most Powerful Planets

The seven planets signify seven days of the week, and connection with each planet is achieved by wearing its correct gemstone. Using your lucky day of the week, you can determine which planet has the luckiest influence on you and which gemstone you should wear or carry close to your body to attract the good luck of that planet. Start wearing the gem on your lucky day and empower with incense and mantras before wearing.

The SUN is the planet of Sunday

This is the principal planet which gives light and warmth, brings fame and recognition and enhances one's personal aura. It is an empowering planet that brings nobility, dignity and power. This gemstone enhances your leadership qualities and increases your levels of confidence so your mind is untroubled and clear. The color that activates the SUN is RED, so all red-colored gemstones are excellent for those of you having SUNDAY as your lucky day based on your Lunar Mansion.

Rubies, red garnets, rubellites or even **red glass** or **crystal** would be extremely powerful. You can also wear red clothes, carry red handbags to enhance the energy of the Sun, but a red gemstone is the most powerful... Start wearing on a Sunday at sunrise after reciting the mantra here 7 times.

Mantra: *Om Grini Suraya Namah Hum Phat*

The MOON is the planet of Monday

The moon has a powerful influence on your mind, your thoughts and attitudes. Lunar energy is associated with the tides and with water, bringing enormous good fortune to those who successfully activate its positive influences; and is especially suitable for those whose lucky day is Monday.

For energizing lunar energy, the best is to wear the pearl, those created in the deep seas or from the freshwater of rivers. Wearing pearls (any color) bring good habits to the wearer and creates good thoughts. It brings calm, peace of mind, mental stability and good health. It also brings wealth and enhances all positive thoughts. Over time, it engenders the respect of others. Start wearing on a Monday in the evening before sunset and recite the mantra here 11 times.

Mantra: *Om Som Somaya Namah Hum Phat*

The Planet MARS rules Tuesday

This is a masculine planet associated with fiery energy and the power of oratory. Activating Mars brings an authoritative air of leadership and confidence like a general leading troops to war. It brings success and victory in any competitive situation. Worn on a Tuesday, a gemstone that resonates with Mars unleashes all its fiery strength in competitive situations. The most powerful gemstone to activate Mars is **natural red coral**, the deeper the red, the better it will be. Start wearing on a Tuesday one hour after sunrise and after reciting the mantra here 19 times.

Mantra: *Om Ang Anghara Kaya Namah Hum Phat*

The Planet MERCURY rules Wednesdays

To anyone who can successfully activate Mercury, this planet brings great intelligence and amazing analytical capabilities that become vastly enhanced. Mercury increases your ability to learn and your powers of absorption are magnified. The ability to memorize also improves. Mercury facilitates powers of expression and communication. You will work fast and become effective in getting things done. The cosmic color of Mercury is green; **emeralds, green tourmalines, green quartz** are all suitable. **Green jade** is the most powerful energizer of Mercury. Anyone wearing jade will always be smarter than others and can always outwit anyone. It is a very powerful gemstone. Start wearing on a Wednesday two hours after sunrise and recite the mantra here 9 times.

Mantra: *Om Bhrum Buddhaya Namah Hum Phat*

The Planet Jupiter rules Thursdays

The most auspicious of the seven planets, this planet attracts wealth and brings great influence to those who can successfully activate its powerful energies. To do so requires you to perform many charitable works and then you will need to wear the gemstone of Jupiter that will make you rise to spectacular heights of success. You will become a highly respected leader wielding power and great influence.

Jupiter's energies are transmitted through yellow gemstones the most powerful of which are **yellow sapphires, citrines, topaz** or **flawless yellow-coloured glass** or **crystal**. Wear a yellow sapphire that is flawless and is at least 7 carats big. This brings enormous wealth luck. **Yellow Citrines** or **Imperial Topaz** are also effective. But they must be flawless or you will be quick-tempered and hard to please. Start wearing on a Thursday an hour before sunset after reciting the mantra here 19 times.

Mantra: *Om Bhrim Bhrihas Pataye Namah Hum Phat*

The Planet Venus rules Fridays

This is the planet of love, romance, sexuality, marriage, material comforts, domestic bliss and luxury. Venus brings all kinds of artistic skills to those whose lucky day is Friday and also to those who empower Venus by connecting to it via the wearing of its gemstones. Venus transmits its cosmic energy through flawless diamonds, quartz crystals, zircons, white sapphires, and other colorless gemstones with clear transparency.

Various subtle hues such as pink, yellow and blue tints are suitable for different types of professions and social positions, as long as the gem does not have any solid color. So it is crystalline stones that resonate best with Venus. Start wearing on a Friday at sunrise after you recite the mantra here 16 times.

Mantra: *Om Shum Shukraya Namah Hum Phat*

The Planet Saturn rules Saturdays

This planet governs careers and an empowered or energized Saturn is excellent for overcoming obstacles at the work place. When projects or bosses cause you to stumble or when hindrances stand in the way, it is because Saturn has to be appeased. Those whose lucky day is Friday possess the ability to rise above hardships and obstacles, but enhancing Saturn by wearing its gemstone will empower you even more. Anyone wearing Blue Sapphires can connect directly with Saturn.

Start wearing on a Saturday 2 and a half hours before sunset and recite the mantra here 23 times.

Mantra: *Om Sham Shanay Scaraya Namah Hum Phat*

So, What Do You Think?

We hope you enjoyed this book and gained some
meaningful insights about your own personal
horoscope and animal sign... and you've put some
of our feng shui recommendations into practice!
Hopefully you are already feeling a difference
and enjoying the results of the positive actions
you have taken.

But Don't Stop Now!

You can receive the latest weekly news and
feng shui updates from Lillian herself absolutely
FREE! Learn even more of her secrets and
open your mind to the deeper possibilities of
feng shui today.

Lillian too's free online weekly ezine is
now AVAILABLE

Here's how easy it is to subscribe:
Just go online to www.lilliantoomandalaezine.com
and sign up today!

Your newsletter will be delivered automatically to your website.

And there's more!

When you subscribe to my FREE Mandala Weekly Ezine you will receive a special personalized BONUS report from me... but it's only available for those who register online at www.lilliantoomandalaezine.com!

DON'T BE LEFT OUT! Join Today!

Thank you for investing in yourself and in this book. Join me online every week and learn how easy it is to make good feng shui a way of life!